MARRIED FOREVER

The Four Seasons of Marriage -

65 years

MARRIED FOREVER – The Four Seasons of Marriage – 65 Years
Written by David Selley
In *MARRIED FOREVER – The Four Seasons of Marriage*, David Selley shares a heartfelt reflection on his 65-year journey with Sonja. Through love's early spark, life's chaotic middle years, and the quiet strength of growing old together, David explores the joys, challenges, and wisdom gained from building a marriage that lasts. Each season offers a new lesson—and this book invites readers to find their own rhythm through every stage of commitment.
First Edition: 2025

Other Books in the PAPA Series and Beyond:
Book 1 – *PAPA #1: The Boy in England – Growing Up Tough*
Book 2 – *PAPA #2: The Young Man in Canada – Grit, Growth & Greatness*
Book 3 – *PAPA #3: The Businessman and Entrepreneur in the USA*
Book 4 – *The Entrepreneur: Papa's Secrets #4*
Book 13 –GenMar – Generational Marketing Strategy – Basket to Casket Marketing 101

Additional books in the PAPA Series are forthcoming. See page 149 for all new titles.

Publisher: Promptings Publishing - Fran Jessee has dedicated herself to bringing David Selley's PAPA Series to life. With meticulous attention to detail, Fran has edited and formatted David's Series to ensure that David's voice shines through on every page. Her commitment to preserving the authenticity of his narrative while enhancing readability makes this book a true reflection of David's experiences. For further information contact franjessee@gmail.com

Cover Design: David Selley
ISBN: 979-8-9916760-7-6
Printed in the United States of America

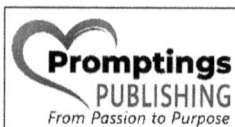

Promptings
PUBLISHING
From Passion to Purpose

May You Have

May your spring bring love in bloom,

With dreams to chase and hearts in tune.

May your summer shine with endless light,

Building memories both day and night.

May your autumn teach you to embrace,

The beauty of change, the gentlest grace.

May your winter wrap you in its glow,

A love that deepens as time does flow.

Through every season, may you find,

A bond that grows, heart and mind.

Together as one, steadfast and true,

Through all of life, may love guide you..

Aloha! From beautiful Hawaii!

David Selley

Dedication

To my wife, Sonja—

There's no way to capture 65 years in a few paragraphs, but this book wouldn't exist—*we* wouldn't exist without you.

You were the one who stayed steady when life threw us curveballs. The one who kept us connected when the road got bumpy. And, let's be honest, the one who held this marriage together more than once, especially when *I* was the one making things difficult. Somehow, you always knew when to hold firm, when to speak softly, and when to just put something good on the table and let it cool us both down.

From the very beginning, there was something different about you. I felt it before I could explain it. There was attraction, of course—but what grew from that was deeper than I ever expected. A lasting romance built on real life, not just the sweet parts, but the messy ones too. You brought kindness, patience, and a kind of calm I didn't know I needed. You've always been the heart of our home and the strength behind our family.

You raised our children with love and wisdom. You kept the bills paid, the meals warm, the schedules moving, and the chaos in check. And while I was busy building things, breaking things, and trying new ideas—you were building something far more lasting: a life, a marriage, a home.

There were times when I look back and wonder how we made it. And then I remember: we made it because *you* made it possible. You were the glue when I was all elbows. You were the light when I got lost in my own plans.

You are, without question, a divine gift in my life. And I say that not as a figure of speech—but as truth. If I ever did one thing right, it was holding onto you.

This book may be about the seasons of marriage, but you're the reason I weathered all of mine.

With all my love,
David

Foreword

When you've been married for 65 years, people assume you have all the answers. They imagine candlelit dinners, endless patience, and synchronized snoring. They think we cracked some secret code that makes love last.

Here's the truth: we didn't crack a code. We just never gave up.

Marriage isn't built on perfection—it's built on quiet resilience, shared laughter, and the decision to keep showing up, even on the days you'd rather hide in the garage.

This book isn't a fairy tale. It's a weather report. It's about the sunshine and storms, the long droughts, the unexpected rainbows, and the surprising moments that made it all worthwhile.

Whether you're newly married, decades in, or still deciding if someone's worth sharing a thermostat with, I hope this story helps you feel a little more seen—and a little more hopeful.

Lasting love isn't about getting it right. It's about staying in it together, season after season.

- David Selley
Author, Husband, and Occasional Wallpaper Assistant

Before We Begin . . .

Choosing a Partner
Who Can Weather the Journey

If there's one thing I've learned after 65 years of marriage, it's this: who you marry matters more than you can imagine.

People like to believe love is enough. That if you just find "the one," everything else will fall into place. But let me tell you—love alone won't carry you through the years. It's the person you choose that makes all the difference.

When I first saw Sonja, I was captivated. She was graceful, beautiful, and confident—even in bright pink ski pants. But it wasn't just attraction that made me realize she was *the one*. It was something deeper. She had kindness, resilience, and a giving spirit—qualities that wouldn't just make our early days exciting but would carry us through the tough seasons ahead.

Because marriage, just like life, has seasons.

There's the Spring of love and new beginnings, when everything feels effortless and full of promise. The Summer of growth and challenges, when careers, kids, and responsibilities demand more than you ever expected. The Autumn of transition, when life shifts, and you're forced to adjust. And finally, the Winter of reflection, when you look back and realize the most important thing wasn't how you started—it was how you stayed together through it all.

That's why choosing the right partner isn't about who makes your heart race in the beginning—it's about choosing someone who will:

- Walk beside you in every season—not just when life is easy, but when it's hard.

- Grow with you instead of against you—because people change, and marriage is about choosing each other *again and again*.

It's easy to fall in love in Spring. But the real question is: Will this person stand with you through the heat of Summer? Through the changes of Autumn? Through the stillness of Winter?

I didn't have all the answers when I married Sonja. But I knew this: I had found someone who wouldn't just be my wife—she would be my partner through every season ahead.

Marriage isn't just about where you begin—it's about how you continue the journey together.

And that's exactly what we're going to explore next.

INTRODUCTION

THE SEASONS OF MARRIAGE

Sixty-five years. That's how long my wife and I have been walking this incredible journey called marriage. And in that time, I've come to see marriage as a reflection of the seasons—a cycle of growth, change, and renewal.

Just like nature, every marriage experiences Spring's fresh beginnings, Summer's warmth and challenges, Autumn's shifting colors, and Winter's quiet strength and reflection. Each season brings its own unique beauty, its own struggles, and its own lessons.

But here's the thing—the seasons don't just happen to you. They're shaped by the choices you make.

Spring is where it all begins, full of new love and possibilities. Summer is where you build and grow, navigating the challenges that come with juggling careers, children, and all the demands life throws your way. Autumn brings change—sometimes exciting, sometimes difficult—but always an opportunity to reflect and adjust as a couple. And Winter? Far from being the end, it's about deepening love, drawing strength from one another, and leaving a legacy that lasts beyond you.

This book is designed to guide you through each of these seasons. I'll share the joys and pitfalls that come with every phase, offering personal stories from my own marriage—what worked, what didn't, and what we learned along the way. You'll also find practical tools, like the 95/5 technique and the 10-point emotional scale, designed to help you communicate better, resolve conflicts, and build a love that can weather any storm.

Marriage isn't about perfection—it's about partnership. It's about understanding that just as seasons change, so do we. The key is learning to embrace those changes together, to grow stronger through them, and to find joy in every stage of the journey.

So whether you're just starting out in the Spring of your marriage or reflecting on decades together in Winter, this book is for you.

Let's step into the seasons of marriage together. My hope is that this book will be more than just advice—it will feel like sitting down with an old friend who understands the ups and downs and wants to share a lifetime of lessons to help you build a marriage that lasts.

Because love isn't just something you fall into.

It's something you grow, season by season.

spring summer autumn winter

This book is for anyone who wants to strengthen their marriage, actually enjoy their time together, and maybe even figure out why your spouse still loads the dishwasher *that* way after all these years. Whether you're looking to reconnect, laugh more, or just survive the thermostat wars, you'll find wisdom, humor, and practical ways to keep love thriving—no matter what season you're in.

Not Married Yet?

Not married yet but checking things out? Welcome! This book isn't just for couples who've been together for decades. Whether you're new to love, preparing for marriage, or just curious about what lies ahead, you'll find insights, humor, and practical wisdom for every stage of the journey.

Marriage, like the seasons, is always changing. Knowing which season you're in can help you navigate it with more grace, humor, and love.

Which season of marriage are you in?

SPRING

"We're still figuring this whole marriage thing out, full of excitement and occasional 'Oops, I didn't know you hated onions that much' moments."

→ Begin with Spring: **New Beginnings – Pg. 11**

SUMMER

"We're in the thick of life—careers, kids, responsibilities, and trying to remember the last time we had a quiet dinner."

→ Head to the Summer Chapter:
Balancing Love and Life's Chaos- Pg. 35

AUTUMN

"Things are changing—kids are growing up (or out), retirement is on the horizon, and we're figuring out our next chapter together."

→ Check out the Autumn Chapter:
Embracing Change Together – Pg. 63

WINTER

"We've been together long enough to finish each other's sentences, bicker about the thermostat, and wonder where we left our glasses."

→ Flip to the Winter Chapter:
Keeping the Fire Burning – Pg. 95

Prefer a Quick-Glance Chart?
Here's Your Season Selector:

Season	Signs You're Here	Go To This Chapter
Spring Pg.11	New to marriage, still learning each other's quirks, filled with excitement (and the occasional minor disaster).	New Beginnings
Summer Pg. 33	Busy schedules, raising kids, juggling careers, trying to make time for each other.	Balancing Love and Life's Chaos
Autumn Pg. 61	Adjusting to life changes—empty nest, career shifts, thinking about the future.	Embracing Change Together
Winter Pg. 91	Deep connection, strong companionship, some new challenges (and plenty of laughs).	Keeping the Fire Burning

Final Thought

"No matter what season you're in, don't skip the journey. You may relate to one chapter now, but every season has wisdom, humor, and lessons worth reading—because love, like the weather, is always changing."

This book is part of David Selley's PAPA Book Series

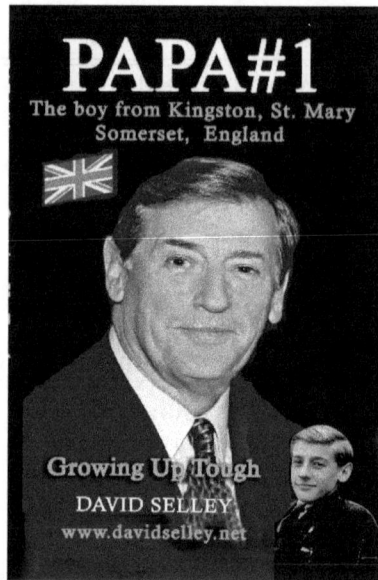

—A 13-book collection of memoirs, relationsip wisdom, entrepreneurship and the International Entrepreneurs Assocation. As part of his Guinnes World Record attempt to become the oldest author to publish the most books in one year. This series spans his journey across England, Canada and the USA. From overcoming hardships to building businesses and sustaining a 65-year marriage, these books capture the humor, resilience and wisdom of a life-well-lived.

TABLE OF CONTENTS

TABLE OF CONTENTS *(continued)*

TABLE OF CONTENTS *(continued)*

Bringing the Stories to Life

Throughout this book, you'll come across a mix of original photographs and illustrations created with the help of modern technology. While I haven't marked every original photo, you'll be able to recognize them by their authentic look and feel. The illustrations are there to fill in the gaps—bringing to life the moments, places, and experiences where no photos were taken. I've done my best to make sure these images reflect the time period as accurately as possible, capturing the spirit of the journey. By blending real photos with visual recreations, I hope to give you a more vivid, immersive look into the stories and history I've shared, as if you're seeing it all through my own eyes.

Welcome –

— to a journey through the four seasons—not the ones with snow shovels and sunscreen, but the seasons of marriage. Yes, marriage has its own climate system, complete with sunny days, occasional storms, and those peculiar stretches where you wonder if you've accidentally packed for the wrong trip.

In this book, we'll explore how marriage cycles through Spring, Summer, Fall and Winter—not necessarily in that order and sometimes all in the same week. My name is David Selley, and I'm here to share not just insights but the humorous, eye-rolling, "Did that really happen?" moments from my own adventures in matrimony. Spoiler alert: marriage doesn't come with a weather forecast, but with the right perspective, even the blizzards can be entertaining.

Think of this as your guidebook to understanding the quirks and surprises that each season brings. It's about embracing the warmth of Spring, the heat of Summer, the changes of Fall, and yes, even the frosty charm of Winter. We'll laugh, reflect, and maybe—just maybe—you'll discover new ways to enjoy the ride, no matter the weather.

So grab a cup of tea (or something stronger if you're in Winter), and let's dive into the seasons of marriage. Trust me, it's going to be a fun, insightful, and compelling adventure—minus the frostbite.

--David Selley, Author

Every Love Story Has a Beginning

Every marriage starts with a story. Ours began with a periwinkle dress and a pair of pink ski pants.

It was an ordinary afternoon, and I was sitting in the upstairs office of the fire hall, looking out the window. Across the street, I saw her. A petite blonde, graceful, confident, and unaware she had just stolen my attention. She wore a blue and white periwinkle dress, standing outside the phone company where she worked, waiting patiently for a ride home.

I didn't know her name. I didn't know her story. But I knew I wanted to.

A few days later, fate (or maybe divine intervention) stepped in. I was on my way to Red Mountain for Friday night skiing, driving my prized black '56 Mercury. Just ahead, I spotted a flash of bright pink ski pants moving with the same graceful confidence I had noticed before. I didn't even have to think. I pulled up, offered her a ride, and in that moment, our love story began on a snowy mountain road.

That night, we talked and laughed, skied under the stars, and unknowingly started a journey that would last a lifetime.

When You Know, You Know

We dated casually at first—weekend ski trips, time at Christina Lake, and a few spontaneous adventures. But something about Sonja felt different from anyone I had met before.

She had a quiet strength, a kindness that wasn't forced, and a way of making life seem easier, even when it wasn't. She laughed at my jokes, even when they weren't that funny. She challenged me without being confrontational and always carried herself with a steady grace that made me want to be better.

After a few months of dating and learning about each other, I realized I wasn't just falling in love—I was building a foundation for a life together.

That's when I knew: this is the person I want by my side, through every season ahead.

The Proposal: A Birthday Surprise

If I had been more romantic and calculated, maybe I would have planned an elaborate proposal—roses, candlelight, and a sunset view. But that's not how life works sometimes.

Instead, on her 21st birthday, I picked her up from work and drove a whole 200 feet into the company parking lot before blurting out, *"Will you marry me?"*

I didn't have a speech prepared. There was no grand setting. Just a diamond ring, a racing heart, and a man who was absolutely sure he had found his forever.

She said yes.

At that moment, I didn't know that our first few minutes as an engaged couple would include two flat tires and a broken car, thanks to my overconfidence in handling railroad tracks. But if we could survive that moment laughing, I figured we could survive a lifetime together.

DAVID & SONJA

A Wedding to Remember

Mr. and Mrs. Erling Dahl
request the honour of your presence
at the marriage of their eldest daughter
Sonja Joyce
to
Mr. David Henry Solley
Saturday, December the nineteenth
nineteen hundred and fifty-nine
at two-thirty in the afternoon
St. Andrew's Anglican Church
Trail, British Columbia

Reception
immediately following
the ceremony
St. Andrew's Parish Hall

R.S.V.P.

Four months later, we stood in St. Andrews Anglican Church in Trail, BC.The moment the wedding march started, I turned to see Sonja walking down the aisle with her father.

"The moment that started our 65-year journey."

For all the buildup of planning, stress, and last-minute details, nothing else mattered in that moment.

The sunlight streaming through the stained-glass windows bathed her in color, casting soft hues across her white dress. It was as if the whole world had been waiting for this moment. I had never seen anything more beautiful.

The wedding itself was simple—just 50 people in the church basemnt for the reception, no extravagant venue, no over-the-top ceremony. And yet, it was perfect.
Because it wasn't the wedding that mattered—it was the commitment.

That was the beginning of a marriage that would last over 65 years, through every season, every challenge, and every moment in between.

Final Thoughts

What Really Matters

Looking back, it's funny how we spend so much time worrying about the perfect proposal, the perfect wedding, and the perfect timing.

But love doesn't follow a script. It unfolds in unexpected moments—on snowy ski hills, over laughter-filled road trips, and even in parking lots.

And in the end, it's not about how extravagant your wedding was or how perfectly your proposal played out.

It's about whether, after decades together, you can still look at each other and say: "I would choose you all oveer again".

David & Sonja
SELLEY

65 Years
Love and Partnership

"I would choose you all over again."

Chapter 1
The Spring of Marriage - New Beginnings

Ah, spring

—the season of fresh starts, blooming flowers, and love so new it still has that "just unwrapped" feeling. This is the time when everything feels possible, when your heart races faster than your brain can keep up, and you're convinced your partner's morning breath smells like roses. (Spoiler alert: it doesn't.)

In the spring of marriage, love is a bit like planting a garden. You're filled with excitement as you scatter seeds everywhere, convinced you'll have a lush, vibrant relationship with zero effort. But here's the catch: just like in gardening, if you don't water it, weed it, and occasionally talk to it (yes, talking to plants works—and it works on spouses too), things start to wither. Suddenly, what you thought was a thriving sunflower turns out to be a dandelion with an attitude problem.

When Sonja and I were in the spring of our marriage, we thought we had it all figured out. We were young, in love, and—let's be honest—a bit clueless. We didn't have much money, but we had each other and an unhealthy amount of confidence that we could conquer the world with little more than charm, stubbornness, and a poorly assembled Collier's Enclopedia bookshelf.

Spring isn't just about beginnings

...it's about growth, discovery, and sometimes realizing that love isn't always effortless. It's about finding joy in the simple things, laughing through the chaos, and learning that even the most beautiful gardens need a little dirt

Every love story has a beginning,

and by now, you've already read ours—the moment a periwinkle dress and a pair of pink ski pants unknowingly changed the course of my life.

At the time, I had no idea that offering a ride to a graceful stranger on a snowy mountain road would lead to a 65-

year journey of love, laughter, and learning. But looking back, I see how those early moments held valuable lessons about love and marriage—lessons that would carry us through every season that followed.

Lesson #1

Love Blooms When You Least Expect It

Spring is full of surprises. You think you're just going skiing, and suddenly you've met the love of your life. The lesson? Stay open. You never know when a simple moment will change your life.

Spring teaches us that love often shows up when you're not looking for it. It's not about finding "the perfect person"—it's about discovering someone who makes the ordinary feel extraordinary.

Boats, Booze and a Brush with Disaster: The Christina Lake Chronicles

After that fateful ski trip, Sonja and I started dating more regularly. We spent weekends at Christina Lake, where I'd show off my pride and joy—a 12-foot runabout boat with an underpowered 25hp outboard engine. It wasn't exactly a speed demon, but it got the job done... most of the time.

One weekend, I was determined to impress my friends with a water skiing demonstration. The boat didn't have enough power to pull someone out of the water the traditional way, so we got creative. The plan? Have the skier sit on the dock, rev the motor, and then yank them into motion.

Sounds simple, right? It was—until the skier's swim trunks snagged on a rusty nail. Imagine being launched into the water with your dignity trailing behind you. It was hilarious for everyone watching... slightly less so for the skier.

This wasn't just about boating. It was about learning that new adventures often come with unexpected surprises—and those surprises are what make the memories stick.

Lesson #2

Growth Comes from New Experiences

Spring is all about trying new things—whether it's skiing, boating, or simply figuring out how to live with another human being who insists on leaving the toilet seat up.

In marriage, you'll face plenty of "firsts." Some will be magical. Some will be messy. But every new experience helps your relationship grow deeper roots.

Story #2
The Great Wallpaper Fiasco
(A Lesson in Teamwork... and Glue)

I'll never forget the time we decided to wallpaper our tiny living room. Now, in theory, this should've been a fun, bonding experience. In reality? It was a test of patience, coordination, and the structural integrity of our marriage.

Picture this: Sonja holding one end of the wallpaper with the precision of a military commander, and me on the other side, attempting to smooth it out like I was wrestling an angry octopus. We didn't have the fancy tools—just a bucket of glue, a sponge that disintegrated halfway through, and an unwavering belief that "how hard could it be?"

Glue was everywhere—on the walls, in our hair, possibly even in places I'm too polite to mention. The wallpaper ended up lopsided, covered in bubbles, and looking like it had survived a small tornado. At one point, I found myself standing on a chair, balancing with one foot, glue dripping down my arm, while Sonja shouted, "IT'S CROOKED!" as if that was the shocking revelation of the century.

But you know what? We laughed. Hard. The kind of laugh that makes your stomach hurt and your face ache. That day, we learned something far more valuable than how to hang wallpaper: teamwork is messy, but it's worth it.

It's not about getting everything perfect. *It's about realizing that sometimes, the glue-covered disasters are the moments you'll cherish the most.*

Story #3
The Road Trip That Should Have Been a Test Drive

Not long after we got married, Sonja and I decided to take a road trip. No GPS, no smartphones—just a paper map, a cooler full of questionable sandwiches, and an unwavering belief that we were "adventurous.

About an hour in, the car broke down. Not the "easy fix" kind of breakdown either. This was the *"why is there smoke coming out of the engine?"* kind.

We sat on the side of the road, baking in the sun, arguing over whose idea this was. But then, something funny happened. We stopped arguing. We looked at each other, sweaty and frustrated, and just burst out laughing. Because what else can you do when life throws you a flat tire and a sunburn?

That's when we realized: it's not the destination that matters—*it's who's sitting next to you when the car breaks down.*

Lesson #3

Don't Confuse Butterflies with a Foundation

Those early relationship butterflies? Lovely. But real love is what's left after the butterflies have flown away and you're still choosing each other—even when the AC is broken, and you're stuck on the side of the road.

Butterflies are fun, but they're fleeting. A strong foundation is built on:

- Shared values
- Mutual respect
- A sense of humor when the car breaks down

Spring marriages often come with a case of what I like to call "relationship spring fever." Everything feels urgent—big decisions, passionate declarations, spontaneous road trips with $5 in your pocket. You're swept up in the thrill, convinced that love alone will carry you through any challenge.

But here's the thing: real love isn't found in perfection—it's found in the messy, imperfect moments. It's in the crooked wallpaper, the burnt dinners, the road trips where you get hopelessly lost but somehow find your way back together.

So, the next time you find yourself knee-deep in a "relationship mess," pause and ask yourself: *"Is this a disaster... or a memory in the making?"*

Reflect, Review, and Grow Together

Now that we've explored the lessons and laughter from the spring of marriage, it's your turn to reflect. Let's take a moment to check in on your relationship's growth and see where new seeds can be planted.

As you've journeyed through the spring of marriage in this chapter, you've read stories about fresh beginnings, unexpected lessons, and the beauty of growth. Now it's your turn to pause and reflect on your own relationship. This test is designed to help you evaluate the foundational elements of your partnership—where you are thriving and where you might need a little more nurturing.

Don't worry—there are no right or wrong answers. Unless your partner's answer is 'I don't know' for everything... in which case, maybe read this chapter again.

Instructions:

- Answer each question honestly, rating from 1 (low) to 10 (high).

- Ideally, both you and your partner should take the test separately, then discuss your answers together in a relaxed setting.

- This is not about judgment; it's a tool for growth, reflection, and meaningful conversation.

Begin –
Spring Relationship Test

1. How is your day-to-day attitude toward your relationship?
   1/2/3/4/5/6/7/8/9/10   (}

2. How intentionally are you nurturing growth in your relationship?
   1/2/3/4/5/6/7/8/9/10   {   }

3. Are you willing to learn and change to make your relationship better?
   1/2/3/4/5/6/7/8/9/10   [   ]

4. Have you read any relationship books or sought new ideas in the last 12 months?
   1/2/3/4/5/6/7/8/9/10   [   ]

5. When was the last time you explored new dreams or plans together?
   1/2/3/4/5/6/7/8/9/10   [   ]

6. How is YOUR health life?
   1/2/3/4/5/6/7/8/9/10   [   ]

7. How is YOUR financial life?
   1/2/3/4/5/6/7/8/9/10   [   ]

8. How is YOUR intimate life?
   1/2/3/4/5/6/7/8/9/10   [   ]

9. How is YOUR romantic life?
   1/2/3/4/5/6/7/8/9/10   [   ]

10. How is YOUR spiritual life?
    1/2/3/4/5/6/7/8/9/10   [   ]

Total Score: _____

Remember, this isn't a scorecard for your marriage—it's a starting point for conversations that matter. Even the strongest gardens need occasional weeding.

Score Interpretation:
- Below 50%: Time to nurture your spring garden! Focus on small daily actions that foster connection.
- 50% to 65%: Growing, but with room for new seeds. Discuss areas where you can water your relationship more intentionally.
- 65% to 85%: Strong roots! Celebrate your

successes, but stay curious about ways to deepen your bond.
- 85% to 100%: Blooming beautifully! Keep tending your relationship with love, laughter, and attention.

Spring Reflection Prompts:
1. What's one "wallpaper moment" you and your partner have had—a challenge that turned into a funny memory?
2. Which area of your relationship surprised you the most in your answers?
3. What's one small change you could make this week to add more joy to your relationship?
4. What are the "butterflies" in your relationship, and what's the foundation beneath them?

Remember: Love, like spring, thrives with attention, care and a little sunshine.

THE
– Emotional –
Richter Scale
OF
OF MARRIAGE

Measuring Life's Quakes

Spring in marriage is full of *firsts*—*first* home together, first time handling finances as a team, *first* time realizing your spouse has a completely different definition of "clean." Everything feels new, exciting, and at times, mildly frustrating.

Like a newly built house settling on its foundation, the first years of marriage come with a few emotional tremors. Some are barely noticeable. Others? Well, let's just say you'll remember them.

Ever notice how some people handle bad news like a stubbed toe, while others act like the world is ending? That's emotions — unpredictable, dramatic, and often hilarious. In business, relationships, and life, we all face emotional tremors. Some pass unnoticed, while others shake our world like a 9.0 earthquake with lasting aftershocks. But fear not! Just as scientists measure the strength of an earthquake, I'm including a foolproof (and slightly ridiculous) way to measure our emotional ups and downs: *The Emotional Richter Scale of Marriage.*

Much like in business, where a single deal can make or break your day, our emotions fluctuate from minor tremors to full-scale disasters. So, grab your emotional hard hat and let's see where you fall on the scale!

Spring Marriage Tremors:
The Early Shakes

Magnitude	Marital Event	Effects
1.0 - 2.0	**The Cute-but-Irritating Discovery**	They leave cabinet doors open. You shut them. No big deal... until it happens every day.
2.1 - 3.0	**The Grocery Store Mismatch**	You shop with a list. They shop like they're on a treasure hunt. A small but telling moment.
3.1 - 4.0	**The *"I Thought You Knew"* Miscommunication**	One assumed the other was handling the bill, appointment, or dinner plans. The response: "I never heard you say that."

Magnitude	Marital Event	Effects
4.1 - 5.0	The First *"How Do You Fold Towels Like That?"* Disagreement	You grew up folding them one way. They do it another. Someone is clearly wrong.
5.1 - 6.0	The Temperature Battle Begins	One of you likes the house at a cozy 75°F. The other wants an ice cave. A thermostat war is inevitable.
6.1 - 7.0	The First *"Just Drop It"* Argument	A minor disagreement that somehow spirals into **silent car rides and deep sighs**.
7.1 - 8.0	The First Big Purchase Surprise	They come home with a new gadget, piece of furniture, or pet. You say, "Oh...we're doing this now?"
8.1 - 9.0	The First Time One of You Sleeps on the Couch	No one remembers exactly *why* the argument started, but pride keeps both sides holding their ground.
9.1 - 10.0	The First "What Have We Done?" Moment	It passes, but for a few hours, you both question if merging two completely different humans into one life was a *smart* idea.

The 95/5 Technique

A Simple Shift for Stronger Relationships

Focus on What Matters Most

Now that you've reflected on your relationship's growth, let me introduce you to one of the simplest yet most powerful tools Sonja and I used throughout our 65+ years of marriage: the 95/5 Technique. It's not just advice—it's a mindset shift that can transform how you handle challenges, big or small.

What Is the 95/5 Technique?

- 95% of the Problem Is Not the Problem.
- 5% Is What Actually Matters.

In relationships, we often focus on the wrong 95%—the petty annoyances, the tone of voice, the unwashed dishes—while ignoring the real 5%, which is usually about deeper feelings: respect, understanding, and connection.

The 95%:
Surface issues (petty arguments, misunderstandings, minor annoyances).

The 5%:
Core emotional needs (feeling valued, heard, respected, or loved).

A Real-Life Example

Imagine Sonja and me wallpapering our tiny living room—a task that nearly turned into an Olympic sport. We argued over crooked lines, glue blobs, and whether 'eyeballing it' was an actual measuring technique. But here's the thing: the crooked wallpaper wasn't the problem (95%). The real issue (5%)? We both wanted to feel heard and appreciated while doing something together.

How to Apply the 95/5 Technique:

1. Pause: When conflict arises, take a breath.
2. Ask: *"What's the 5% here? What really matters?"*
3. Shift Focus: Instead of fixing the surface issue, address the underlying emotional need.
4. Respond, Don't React: Speak to the heart of the issue with kindness and clarity.

Interactive Activity: Finding the 5%

- Think of a recent disagreement with your partner.
- Write down what the argument was about (the 95%).
- Now ask: *"What was the real issue beneath it?"* (the 5%).
- Reflect together: *"How could we have handled it differently focusing on the 5%?"*

The 95/5 Technique Across All Seasons:

- Spring: Identify the 5% in new experiences and early misunderstandings.
- Summer: Apply it to handle the heat of life's busyness, parenting stress, or work conflicts.
- Autumn: Use it to navigate change, transitions, and shifting dynamics in the relationship.
- Winter: Reflect on it to deepen connection, resolve lingering issues, and focus on legacy.

Remember: It's not about winning arguments; it's about winning each other's hearts, one mindful moment at a time.

The "Spring Fever" Journal

Write down three things you thought would be easy in your relationship—but turned out to be hilariously complicated. What did those moments teach you?

Then, flip the script:

- List three things you thought would be hard—but turned out to be surprisingly simple.

- But maybe it's time for a spontaneous adventure to bring back that springtime spark.

Our Spring Garden

1. **Planting Seeds:**
   Draw or list the *"seeds"* you planted in your relationship during your first year together. These could be **values, dreams, hopes, traditions, trust**, or **goals**—the foundational things you nurtured to help your relationship grow.

2. **Pulling Weeds:**
   Identify the *"weeds"* you've had to pull along the way. What early habits, misunderstandings, or challenges did you need to overcome to create a healthier connection?

3. What's Blooming Now?

Reflect on the parts of your relationship that have continued to grow and thrive over time. What's still *blooming* beautifully in your garden of love?

4. *Positive Seeds*

(Things You Nurture Together):

- ✓ Goals
- ✓ Hopes
- ✓ Beliefs
- ✓ Traditions
- ✓ Commitment
- ✓ Memories
- ✓ Trust
- ✓ Passions
- ✓ Intentions
- ✓ Connections
- ✓ Principles
- ✓ Ambitions
- ✓ Respect
- ✓ Kindness
- ✓ Laughter
- ✓ Patience
- ✓ Gratitude
- ✓ Compromise
- ✓ Shared Interests
- ✓ Adventures
- ✓ Security
- ✓ Joy
- ✓ Communication
- ✓ Affection

Spring Takeaways

1. ***Slow Down and Smell the Roses (Before You Trip Over them):***
   It's tempting to sprint through the early days, but the best relationships are marathons, not sprints. Take time to enjoy the small moments.

2. ***Teamwork: Not Always Pretty, But It's Essential:***
   Whether you're hanging wallpaper or navigating life's bigger challenges, remember that it's not about perfection—it's about partnership.

3. ***Don't Confuse Butterflies with a Foundation::***
   Those early relationship butterflies? Lovely. But real love is what's left after the butterflies have flown away and you're still choosing each other.

Chapter 2

The Summer of Marriage – Balancing Love & Life's Chaos

Ah, summer

—the season of warmth, growth, and those moments where love feels both effortless and tested. If spring was about fresh beginnings and butterflies, summer is where the real work begins. This is the time when marriages truly take root, where the seeds planted in spring begin to flourish. But just like a summer garden, it requires care, attention, and yes, sometimes a little weeding.

It's the time when relationships are like gardens: you've planted the seeds, but now comes the watering, weeding, and the occasional battle with unexpected storms.

In the summer of marriage, life can feel both vibrant and overwhelming. Careers are in full swing, children may enter the picture, and the honeymoon phase starts to fade, replaced by the reality of daily responsibilities. This is where the real work of partnership begins— navigating life's demands while keeping the connection alive.

When Sonja and I entered the summer of our marriage, again, we thought we had it all figured out by this time. We had survived the excitement of spring, convinced that love alone would carry us through. But summer had different lessons to teach—about patience, teamwork, and the importance of showing up even when it's not easy.

Story # 1
The Heat of Responsibility

Summer often brings the heat—not just from the sun but from the pressures of work, family, and personal growth. Sonja and I faced this when we bought our first home. Suddenly, we were juggling mortgage payments, career ambitions, and household chores. The excitement of new beginnings was replaced by the daily grind of "adulting."

One evening, after a particularly exhausting day, we found ourselves arguing over something trivial—whose turn it was to do the dishes. It wasn't really about the dishes; it was about feeling overwhelmed and unappreciated. That night, we realized the importance of small gestures—a thank you, a hug, a simple acknowledgment of each other's efforts.

Lesson #1
Balancing Life and Love

Lesson: It's not the big romantic gestures that sustain a marriage; it's the daily acts of kindness and appreciation.

Story #2

The Great Camping Catastrophe
(A Lesson in Adaptability)

One summer, Sonja and I decided to take the kids on a camping trip. It was supposed to be an idyllic escape into nature, complete with campfires, s'mores, and starry nights. We packed the car with military precision, convinced we had everything we needed.
Spoiler alert: we didn't.

The tent had a hole the size of a grapefruit, the bug spray mysteriously vanished, and it rained. Not a gentle drizzle, but a full-blown, tent-collapsing, mud-sliding downpour. The kids were miserable, we were soaked, and the marshmallows floated away like tiny sugary rafts.

But here's the thing—we laughed. Not right away, of course. First, there was frustration, some colorful language, and a silent agreement that we were never doing this again. But later, as we huddled under a makeshift tarp, sharing soggy sandwiches, we found the humor in it all. That disastrous trip became one of our favorite family stories.

Lesson #2

Adaptability is the Key to Survival

Marriage, like camping, rarely goes as planned. The ability to adapt, to laugh in the face of soggy sandwiches and metaphorical rainstorms, is what keeps the relationship strong. It's not about having a perfect plan; it's about rolling with the punches and finding joy in the chaos.

Story #3

The Barbecue Blow-Up
(A Lesson in Communication)

Another summer memory involves a neighborhood barbecue. I was in charge of the grill, feeling like the king of charcoal, while Sonja handled everything else— setting the table, managing the kids, and trying not to strangle me with a spatula.

Somewhere between flipping burgers and sipping a cold drink, I missed the subtle signs of her growing frustration. It wasn't until she snapped, "Must be nice to relax while I do everything else," that I realized I'd been blissfully unaware of how unevenly the workload was divided.

Lesson #3

Speak Up Before You Boil Over

In marriage, unspoken frustrations are like unattended grills—eventually, something's going to catch fire. Open communication, even about the small stuff, prevents resentment from simmering beneath the surface. It's okay to ask for help, and it's even more okay to offer it before being asked.

Story #4

The Road Trip Reckoning
(A Lesson in Patience)

One summer, we decided to take a cross-country road trip. Picture this: two adults, two restless kids, a car packed tighter than a can of sardines, and a playlist stuck on repeat because someone (me) forgot to download new songs. This wasn't the first time music failed us on a long drive. Back in the day—before Spotify and playlists—our road trip soundtrack came from a worn-out cassette collection. You haven't truly suffered until you've heard the same side of a mixed tape play for six hours straight because someone forgot to flip it. Modern problems, meet vintage frustrations.

By day three, patience was in short supply. The kids were arguing over invisible lines in the backseat, and Sonja and I were arguing over who was more exhausted. But somewhere between the endless highways and questionable roadside diners, we found a rhythm. We learned to take turns being the calm one, to find humor in the absurd, and to appreciate the journey even when the destination felt far away.

Lesson #4
Patience is a Team Sport

Marriage isn't about never getting frustrated; it's about how you handle it together. Taking turns being the patient one, offering grace when the other person is struggling, and remembering that you're on the same team can turn even the most stressful situations into bonding experiences.

Story #5

The Garden That Grew Us
(A Lesson in Growth)

Sonja loved gardening. I, on the other hand, believed plants should fend for themselves. But one summer, she roped me into creating a vegetable garden. We planted, watered, weeded, and waited. And waited.

At first, it was frustrating. Nothing seemed to grow fast enough, and I was ready to declare the whole project a failure. But Sonja taught me that growth takes time, both in gardens and in relationships. By the end of the summer, we had more than vegetables; we had a new appreciation for patience, teamwork, and the quiet joy of watching something thrive because we nurtured it together.

Lesson #5

Growth Requires Consistent Care

Relationships, like gardens, need regular attention. Love isn't a "set it and forget it" deal. It's the small, consistent acts of care that make the biggest difference over time. Water it with kindness, pull out the weeds of misunderstanding, and celebrate the little blooms along the way.

Conclusion
The Warmth Beneath the Heat

Summer in marriage is about embracing the heat—both the warmth of deep connection and the challenges that test your resilience. It's about growing together, weathering the storms, and finding joy in the messy, beautiful process of building a life side by side.

So, whether you're navigating road trips, garden failures, or barbecue blow-ups, remember: summer isn't just a season. It's a testament to your commitment, your growth, and the love that flourishes when you nurture it, even on the hottest days.

SUMMER

Reflect, Review and Grow Together

Now that we've basked in the warmth and growth of the summer of marriage, it's your turn to reflect. Let's take a moment to celebrate the fruits of your relationship's hard work and see where you might need to water and tend a little more.

As you've journeyed through the summer of marriage in this chapter, you've read stories about deepening connections, navigating challenges under the heat of life, and savoring the richness of love in full bloom. Now it's your turn to pause and reflect on your own relationship. This exercise is designed to help you evaluate the strength of your partnership—where your love is thriving and where it might need a little extra shade or attention.

Don't worry—there are no right or wrong answers. Unless your partner's answer is, 'Wait... we're supposed to water this relationship?' In that case, maybe take a break, grab some lemonade, and read this chapter again. Instructions:

- Answer each question honestly, rating from 1 (low) to 10 (high).
- Ideally, both you and your partner should take the test separately, then discuss your answers together in a relaxed setting.
- This is not about judgment; it's a tool for growth, reflection, and meaningful conversation.

Begin – Summer Relationship Check-In

1. How well do you and your partner handle stress and busy schedules together?
   1/2/3/4/5/6/7/8/9/10   {   }

2. How effectively do you communicate your needs during challenging times?
   1/2/3/4/5/6/7/8/9/10   [   ]

3. Are you both making time to nurture your connection despite daily responsibilities?
   1/2/3/4/5/6/7/8/9/10   [   ]

4. Do you actively support each other's personal growth and ambitions?
   1/2/3/4/5/6/7/8/9/10   [   ]

5. When was the last time you shared a meaningful experience or adventure together?
   1/2/3/4/5/6/7/8/9/10   [   ]

6. How well do you balance work, family, and personal time as a couple?
   1/2/3/4/5/6/7/8/9/10   [   ]

7. How secure do you feel in your financial partnership and decision-making?
   1/2/3/4/5/6/7/8/9/10   [   ]

8. How fulfilling is your intimate connection, both emotionally and physically
   1/2/3/4/5/6/7/8/9/10   [   ]

9. How often do you express appreciation and gratitude for each other?
   1/2/3/4/5/6/7/8/9/10   [   ]

10. How aligned are you in your long-term goals and shared vision for the future?
    1/2/3/4/5/6/7/8/9/10

Total Score: _____

Remember:
Love, like summer, flourishes
with care, consistency, and a little shade
when things get too hot.

Don't forget, this isn't a scorecard for your marriage—it's a starting point for conversations that matter. Even the healthiest relationships need regular care and attention.

Score Interpretation:
- Below 50%: Time to water your summer garden! Focus on small, daily actions that nurture connection.
- 50% to 65%: Growing strong but could use some extra sunshine. Identify areas where you can invest more energy.
- 65% to 85%: Vibrant and thriving! Celebrate your successes and explore ways to deepen your bond further.
- 85% to 100%: Flourishing beautifully! Keep tending to your relationship with love, laughter, and intentional growth.

Summer Reflection Prompts:

1. What's one "camping catastrophe" or "barbecue blow-up" moment that turned into a memorable experience?
2. Which area of your relationship surprised you the most in your answers?
3. What's one small change you could make this week to bring more joy and connection into your relationship?
4. How do you and your partner stay connected when life gets busy, and what strategies could you improve?

Communication
in Marriage Changes
Not because people change (though they do), but because life does

In Spring, you talk about everything—you're fascinated by each other, finishing each other's sentences, and staying up late just to chat. In Summer, conversations shift from dreams and big ideas to who's picking up the kids and why there's never enough money in the budget. By Autumn, the house is quieter, and you start to realize... so are your conversations. And in Winter, you begin to wonder if you've said all the things that really matter—or if there's still time to say them.

So pay attention to how communication evolves. Each season comes with new challenges and new ways to connect. And right now*? **We're in Summer—the season of talking while tired.***

Responsibility & Growth
"Talking While Tired"

When you're newly married, conversations just flow—you talk about everything, and somehow, it all feels important. But by the time you hit the Summer of marriage, talking becomes more about logistics than connection.

Instead of deep discussions about life's meaning, you're debating who forgot to take the trash out or why the credit card bill looks suspiciously like someone's been impulse shopping again. By the time you've handled work, kids, and whatever else life throws at you, one of you still wants to talk, and the other is just trying to stay awake.

Let's dig into why one person always seems to have more words left at the end of the day—and what to do about it.

A Marriage Mystery
The 4,000 vs. 1,500 Word Myth

It's been said that women need to "get off" about 4,000 words per day to feel emotionally content, while men only need around 1,500. If true, this might explain why some husbands find themselves staring blankly while their wives enthusiastically recap their day—including what Susan at the office ate for lunch, the latest sale at Target, and how the neighbor's dog has a new sweater.

The difference? Women use words for connection, while men use them for function.

This brings us to another age-old truth:

- Women go shopping. Men go to buy.

A woman might browse, compare, try on, reconsider, and finally purchase something after exploring all the options. A man? He walks into the store, grabs what he came for, and leaves—mission accomplished.

It's not that one way is better than the other; it's just how our brains are wired.

So, the next time you feel like your spouse isn't listening, remember—they may have already hit their 1,500-word limit for the day.

How This Plays Out in Marriage

Time of Day	Her Words (4,000)	His Words (1,500)
Morning Coffee	"Did you sleep well? I had a weird dream. Oh, and I was thinking we should plan a weekend trip…"	"Yeah. Slept fine."
During the Day	Chats with coworkers, calls her sister, texts a friend. 2,500 words down, 1,500 to go.	Work meetings, a couple of emails. 1,200 words used—only 300 left in the tank.

Time of Day	Her Words (4,000)	His Words (1,500)
Dinner Time	"How was your day? Did you talk to your boss? What do you think about repainting the living room?"	"Good. Yeah. Maybe."
Late Evening	"So, about the weekend trip...I was thinking a cabin in the mountains, or maybe the beach? What do you think? Also, what do you think about Warm Earth for the living room? Not too brown, not too beige..."	(Silence. He's completely out of words. Might be asleep.)

See the problem? She's still got words to spend. He's running on empty.

Bridging the Communication Gap

If this sounds familiar, don't panic. It's not a marriage problem—it's a word count problem.

- **If You're the Talker:** Give your spouse some breathing room when they get home. They need a word recharge before they can engage.
- **If You're the Quiet One:** Give your spouse something to work with. Even a simple "Tell me more" can go a long way.
- **For Both of You:** Find a communication rhythm that works. Some couples do daily check-ins,

others have longer conversations once a week. The goal isn't to match word counts—it's to make sure both people feel heard.

The way we communicate changes as life gets busier. Understanding why one person talks more than the other (and how to adjust) can turn everyday conversations into real connection.

SUMMER

The 95/5 Technique

A Simple Shift for Stronger Relationships
Focus on What Matters Most

Now that you've reflected on your relationship's growth, let me introduce you to one of the simplest yet most powerful tools Sonja and I used throughout our 65+ years of marriage: the 95/5 Technique. It's not just advice, it's a mindset shift that can transform how you handle challenges, big or small.

What Is the 95/5 Technique?

- 95% of the Problem Is Not the Problem.
- 5% Is What Actually Matters.

In relationships, we often focus on the wrong 95%—the petty annoyances, the tone of voice, the unwashed dishes—while ignoring the real 5%, which is usually about deeper feelings: respect, understanding, and connection.

The 95%

Surface issues (petty arguments, misunderstandings, minor annoyances).

The 5%

:
Core emotional needs
(feeling valued, heard, respected, or loved).

A Real-Life Example

Imagine Sonja and me trying to manage a chaotic summer barbecue—guests arriving late, burnt burgers, kids running wild. We argued over who forgot the ice, why the grill wouldn't light, and who was supposed to bring the extra chairs. But here's the thing: the forgotten ice wasn't the problem (95%). The real issue (5%)? We both wanted to feel appreciated for the effort we put into making the day special.

How to Apply the 95/5 Technique:

1. Pause: When conflict arises, take a breath.
2. Ask: "What's the 5% here? What really matters?"

3. Shift Focus: Instead of fixing the surface issue, address the underlying emotional need.
4. Respond, Don't React: Speak to the heart of the issue with kindness and clarity.

Interactive Activity: Finding the 5%

- Think of a recent disagreement with your partner.
- Write down what the argument was about (the 95%).
- Now ask: "What was the real issue beneath it?" (the 5%).
- Reflect together: "How could we have handled it differently focusing on the 5%?"

The 95/5 Technique Across All Seasons:

- Spring: Identify the 5% in new experiences and early misunderstandings.
- Summer: Apply it to handle the heat of life's busyness, parenting stress, or work conflicts.
- Autumn: Use it to navigate change, transitions, and shifting dynamics in the relationship.
- Winter: Reflect on it to deepen connection, resolve lingering issues, and focus on legacy.

Remember: It's not about winning arguments; it's about winning each other's hearts, one mindful moment at a time.

Is It Time For A Spontaneous Adventure?

Write down three things in your relationship that felt manageable at first but turned out to be unexpectedly difficult. What lessons did those challenges teach you about partnership?

Then, flip the script:
- List three things you thought would be tough but turned out to be easier than expected.

Plan one small summer-inspired outing together—a sunset drive, a picnic, or a playful day at the beach—to rekindle that warm, adventurous energy in your relationship.

Cultivating Your Summer Garden

1. Nurturing Growth

What are the "seeds" you planted earlier in your relationship that are now flourishing? Consider shared goals, personal dreams, or relationship values that have strengthened over time.

2. Managing the Heat

Summer can bring intensity—whether it's career pressures, parenting challenges, or simply the weight of daily responsibilities. How do you and your partner "water" your relationship to prevent burnout? What strategies help you stay connected during busy seasons?

3. Pulling Weeds

Every relationship picks up a few bad habits along the way—routines that no longer serve you, lingering irritations, or patterns that quietly chip away at connection. This part of summer is about identifying what's getting in the way of growth.

Ask yourselves:

- Are there habits or behaviors we've been ignoring that are causing tension?
- Are we holding on to resentment or unresolved issues that need clearing out?
- What are we willing to release to make room for better connection?

Like any thriving garden, a relationship needs weeding. Pull the small stuff before it takes root.

What are the "seeds" you planted earlier in your relationship that are now flourishing? Consider shared goals, personal dreams, or relationship values that have strengthened over time.

- Are there habits or behaviors we've been ignoring that are causing tension?
- Are we holding on to resentment or unresolved issues that need clearing out?
- What are we willing to release to make room for better connection?

> Like any thriving garden, a relationship needs weeding. Pull the small stuff before it takes root.
>
> **Summer Growth List**

What Keeps Your Relationship Thriving?

- Communication
- Teamwork
- Emotional Support
- Mutual Encouragement
- Time Together
- Trust
- Affection
- Laughter
- Problem-Solving
- Shared Adventures
- Respect
- Acts of Service
- Gratitude
- Relationship Rituals
- Financial Unity
- Intimacy
- Future Planning
- Conflict Resolution: Take a moment to reflect on how you and your partner are growing together this summer. Are there any weeds (bad habits, unresolved conflicts, or neglected areas) that need pulling? What's one way you can intentionally nurture your connection this week?

Summer Takeaways

1. **Embrace the Heat Without Burning Out:**
   Summer in marriage brings intensity—work, family, and commitments can pile up. Take time to cool down and prioritize each other amidst the busyness.

2. **Partnership Over Perfection:**
   Whether managing careers, raising children, or handling responsibilities, remember that teamwork is more important than getting everything right.

3. **Keep the Adventure Alive:**
   Relationships thrive on shared experiences. Make space for fun, spontaneity, and new adventures to keep the connection strong, even in the busiest seasons.

Your relationship is a continuous journey. Keep watering, keep growing, and most importantly—keep enjoying the warmth of your summer together!

Chapter **3**

Autumn in Marriage - Embracing Change Together

Autumn in marriage sneaks up on you. One day, life is a whirlwind of kids, careers, and endless to-do lists. Then suddenly, the house is quieter, the schedule less frantic, and you find yourself sitting across the dinner table from your spouse, thinking, *Well... now what?*

For some, this season feels like a well-earned break—finally, a chance to breathe. For others, it's more like staring at a familiar stranger, wondering when you stopped having real conversations that didn't involve bills, carpools, or fixing the water heater.

Here's the truth: Autumn isn't the beginning of the end—it's the start of something new. This is the season to rediscover why you married each other in the first place. To find new things to talk about, new adventures to share, and maybe even new ways to drive each other just a little crazy (because let's be honest, that never really stops).

Marriage isn't about keeping things the same—it's about growing together through every season. And in Autumn, that means embracing the quieter moments, finding laughter in the little things, and making sure the best years aren't just behind you, but still ahead.

Story # 1

The Career Curveball, Role Reversal

And Learning to Love in a New Way

They say Autumn is the season of change—when the heat of Summer fades, the leaves turn, and everything settles into something quieter, something different. Well, let me tell you, Autumn hit me like a freight train when I walked out of that corporate office for the last time.

One day, I was David Selley, Manager of the Year—leading a team, making executive decisions, and bringing home a steady paycheck. The next? I was David Selley, unemployed husband—standing in my own kitchen with absolutely no idea what to do next.

Now, I'd love to tell you I handled this transition with grace and wisdom, but the truth is, I spent a few days pacing, sighing dramatically, and wondering if the world had just ended.

Meanwhile, Sonja—my wife, my rock—had already been building her business, *Sonja's Food & Gifts.* And while I was in the middle of my personal crisis, she casually mentioned, "Why don't you come help me at the store?" Help her at the store? What was I supposed to do, stock shelves? I had spent decades making deals, managing teams, and building businesses. And now I was supposed to...sell tea and shortbread?

But let me tell you something about Autumn in marriage—this is the season when love asks you to change, whether you like it or not. It's when you stop clinging to who you were and start embracing who you need to be for each other.

The Reality Check
Trading the Suit for an Apron

So, I did it. I showed up at the shop, ready to "help." Within five minutes, I had already put the inventory in the wrong place, confused two customers, and discovered that I had absolutely no idea what I was doing.
Sonja, bless her heart, just smiled and said, "You'll get

there." And that's when I realized—this wasn't about me. It was about her. About our marriage evolving. About me learning how to love in this new season by showing up in a way I never had before.

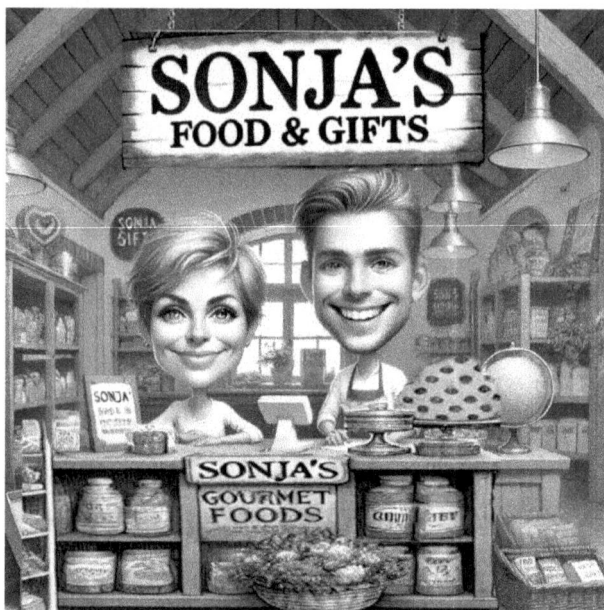

Over time, I figured it out. I learned how to listen instead of lead, how to support instead of take charge. And you know what? I actually loved it—not just the work, but the fact that I was doing it with Sonja, for Sonja.

Because Autumn in marriage? It's not about who you used to be—it's about who you're becoming together.

Lesson #1

Lesson Learned:
Love Evolves When You Do

In the early years, love looks like romance, adventure, and dreaming together. But in Autumn, love looks like being willing to change for each other—to let go of old roles, old ideas, and embrace what's next.

And sometimes, what's next is selling shortbread.

Story #2

The Weekend That Saved Our Marriage

You know what happens in Autumn? The world gets quieter. The leaves stop rustling, the air cools, and suddenly, you notice things you didn't before—like how your house isn't as loud anymore. Or how the conversations with your spouse have somehow gotten... shorter.

It wasn't that Sonja and I weren't talking. We were. Every day.

- "Did you get the mail?"
- "Did you pay the bill?"
- "Are we out of milk?"

But somewhere along the way, the deep conversations, the ones that made us fall in love in the first place, had started to fade.

That's when we went on a marriage retreat. Now, let me tell you something—there's nothing that will make a man sweat faster than a priest telling him he needs to write his wife a 10-minute letter about his true feelings.

The Letter That Nearly Ended It All

So, I did it. I sat down and poured *everything onto that paper*—the good, the bad, the things I never said out loud. And I thought, *this will be great, she'll love it.*

Friends, let me tell you: *I was wrong.*

The moment she read it, I could feel the temperature in the room drop by at least 10 degrees. Her smile faded, her eyes narrowed, and I knew...*I had made a grave mistake.*

That night was *cold.* I'm talking *sleeping-on-the-far-edge-of-the-bed, do-not-breathe-on-me, "I'm fine" kind of cold.*

But the next morning, something happened.

We sat down. We read the letters again. And this time, instead of getting defensive, we started talking. *Really talking.* We had a conversation we hadn't had in *years*— not about logistics, not about schedules, but *about us.*

And by the end of that retreat, it was like we had *found each other all over again.*

Lesson #2

Lesson Learned:
Love Needs New Conversations

Autumn in marriage is dangerous if you stop talking. Not just about what's for dinner, but about what's in your heart.

If you're not careful, one day you'll wake up and realize you don't even know the person sitting across from you. Don't wait for a priest to tell you to write a letter. Start talking now.

AUTUMN

The Season of Reflection and Renewal

As we enter the Autumn of marriage, we find ourselves in a season of change, much like the golden leaves drifting from the trees. The air is crisp, and so is our perspective—this is the time to take stock of our journey together, to laugh at the blunders, appreciate the beauty, and prepare for what's ahead. After all, if we're lucky, we'll be raking in memories instead of just leaves!

This stage of life isn't about resisting change—it's about embracing it, adapting, and, most importantly, enjoying the ride together. With that in mind, let's step back and assess where we are, where we're headed, and how we can make this season even richer.

Autumn Relationship Assessment
Instructions

- Answer each question honestly, rating from 1 (low) to 10 (high).

- Both partners should complete the assessment separately, then come together (preferably over something warm and comforting—like cocoa or cider) to discuss your responses.

- Remember, this is about growth, not grading— unless you plan to frame your score and hang it on the fridge.

1. How well do we adapt to changes and transitions in our lives together? *(Do we embrace change like a crisp autumn breeze, or resist like a tree stubbornly holding onto its last leaf?)*   1/2/3/4/5/6/7/8/9/10   (}

2. How effectively do we communicate our feelings and concerns during seasonal shifts in life? *(Do we share openly like a fall harvest, or keep things bottled up like a forgotten jar of preserves?)*   1/2/3/4/5/6/7/8/9/10   {   }

3. How supportive are we of each other's personal growth and seasonal changes? *(Do we encourage each other like a well-tended autumn garden, or let things wither from neglect?)*   1/2/3/4/5/6/7/8/9/10   {   }

4. How often do we reflect on past experiences and learn from them? *(Do we take stock of what's worked, like a farmer planning for the next planting season, or repeat the same mistakes like leaves circling the drain?)*
   1/2/3/4/5/6/7/8/9/10   { }

5. How do we handle conflicts and disagreements as the seasons of our relationship change? *(Do we address issues like raking up fallen leaves, or let them pile up until they become overwhelming?*
   1/2/3/4/5/6/7/8/9/10   { }

6. How connected do we feel in our daily routines as the days shorten and schedules shift? *(Are we still finding time to walk hand-in-hand, or do we just pass like migrating birds on different paths?)*
   1/2/3/4/5/6/7/8/9/10   { }

7. How satisfied are we with our physical and emotional intimacy as we move into a slower, cozier season? *(Are we drawing closer like a couple under a shared blanket, or drifting apart like fallen leaves in the wind?)*
   1/2/3/4/5/6/7/8/9/10   [ ]

8. How well do we balance our individual needs with our needs as a couple, especially as the pace of life changes? *(Do we make space for 'me' without losing 'we,' or do we get lost in our own to-do lists?)*
   1/2/3/4/5/6/7/8/9/10   [ ]

9. How often do we express gratitude and appreciation for each other during this season of reflection? *(Do we recognize the small things, like the last apple on the tree, or do we take each other for granted, assuming there's always more?)*
     1/2/3/4/5/6/7/8/9/10   [   ]

10. How aligned are we in our future plans and goals as we prepare for the next season together? *(Are we stacking firewood for the winter together, or are we both assuming the other will do it?)*
     1/2/3/4/5/6/7/8/9/10   [   ]

Total Score: _____

Score Interpretation

- **Below 50:** Time to rake in some changes! Focus on communication, reconnection, and shared joy.
- **50 to 65:** A steady relationship, but there's room to deepen your bond—maybe time for a new shared adventure?
- **65 to 85:** A strong foundation! Keep nurturing your connection and discovering new ways to grow together.
- **85 to 100:** You're golden! Like a perfectly aged bottle of wine, your love has depth, richness, and great staying power. Keep savoring the journey!

Autumn Reflection Prompts

1. What recent change or challenge have we faced together, and what did we learn from it?
2. How can we create new traditions that reflect who we are now, rather than who we were years ago?
3. In what ways can we support each other's personal growth in this season of our lives?
4. What are we most grateful for in our relationship right now, and how can we express that appreciation more often?

Final Thought

Autumn is a time of transformation and wisdom. The trick is to enjoy the changes, appreciate the journey, and remember—no matter what season you're in, love is always in bloom when nurtured well.

What's Up Next?

The next four sections are not about reinventing your marriage—but fine-tuning what's already there. Think of it like tending a fall garden: a little pruning, a little watering, and maybe pulling a few weeds before they take over the whole yard.

- Start with **The Great Word Gap** if your conversations have been reduced to "Did you pay the bill?" and "Are we out of milk?" This will help bring back real conversations, not just grocery lists.

- Move into **The 95/5 Technique** to figure out why you're really irritated—because we all know it's usually not about the remote control, the thermostat, or who left crumbs in the butter.

- Dig into **Cultivating Your Autumn Garden** to take stock of what's working, what needs a little tending, and how to keep growing together (without accidentally strangling each other in the process).

- Wrap it all up with **Autumn Reflections: A Journaling Exercise**—a chance to pause, reflect, and maybe even surprise yourself with what you discover about your marriage.

No matter where you start, the goal is simple: Reconnect, laugh a little, and make sure this season of marriage is one you actually enjoy together. And if all else fails...just pour some cider, watch the leaves fall, and blame everything on the squirrels.

THE
Great
Word Gap
IN Marriage

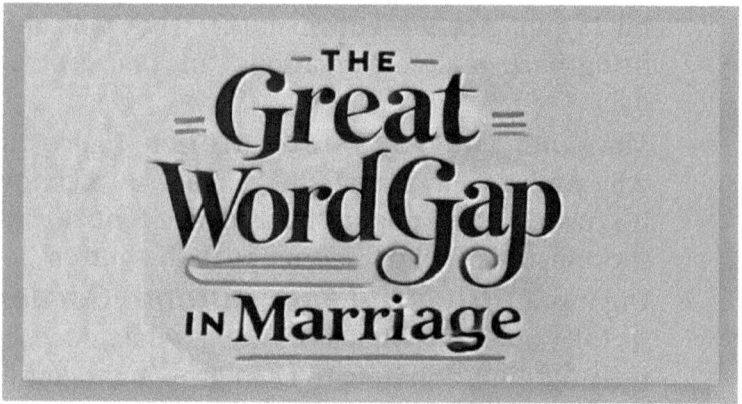

What Happened to All Our Conversations?

This gap isn't about love fading—it's about life shifting. When the daily whirlwind dies down, you may realize you're left with the very person you started this whole journey with. Only now, there's more time to think, to reflect... and to wonder, "What do we talk about now?" Here's the thing: If you don't intentionally bridge the Word Gap, it can become a canyon. And we don't want to be shouting "I love you" across a canyon (especially if one of us has selective hearing).

Strategies to Reconnect (Without Making It Feel Like a Chore)

1. *Make Conversations a Priority (No, Talking About the Weather Doesn't Count)*

Autumn is a season of slowing down—use it as an opportunity to be intentional. Set aside time to talk—not just about errands and the news, but about life. What's on your mind? What dreams have been waiting on the back burner? What's a ridiculous idea you've been too afraid to say out loud?

2. *Create New Adventures (Or Dust Off the Old Ones)*

The air is crisp, the leaves are changing—get outside and do something together. You used to have fun together, remember? Hiking, cooking, trying new things, or even just making fun of bad TV. Pick something and dive back in. A shared laugh does wonders for a relationship.

3. *Listen Like You Actually Want to Know the Answer*

Sometimes, we get so used to each other that we stop really listening. Try this: Ask your partner a question and then zip it. No interrupting, no fixing—just listen. You might be surprised at what you learn.

4. *Reignite Date Nights (Even if It's Just a Backyard Picnic Under the Stars)*

Date nights aren't just for young couples trying to impress each other. They're for reminding you why you chose this person in the first place. The beauty of Autumn makes it easy—bonfires, scenic drives, cozy nights in. It doesn't have to be extravagant—just intentional.

5. Get an Outside Perspective (Before You Start Communicating via Sticky Notes)

If the silence feels heavy, there's no shame in seeking support. A good couples' workshop, a mentor, or even a book that sparks conversation can be a great way to jumpstart connection again.

The Beauty of Autumn: A Season for Deepening, Not Drifting

Just like the changing trees, marriage in Autumn takes on new colors—richer, deeper, and full of character. It's not about mourning what's past; it's about appreciating what's grown over time.

Yes, the noise may have quieted, but that just means there's space to rediscover each other in ways you couldn't before.

So, embrace this season together. Keep the conversations going, keep the laughter alive, and if all else fails—just blame the Word Gap on the squirrels.

AUTUMN

Using The 95/5 Technique
in the Autumn of Marriage

A Season of Change, Connection, and the Occasional
"Why Do You Load the Dishwasher Like That?"

Now we are in autumn—where the air is crisp, the leaves are changing, and somehow, so is your patience. This season of marriage isn't about dramatic reinventions, it's about seeing each other clearly, after years of shifting roles, responsibilities, and routines. By now, you've seen each other through everything from burned dinners to late-night worries about the kids (who may now have their own dinner-burning stories). You know each other well—but that doesn't mean you see everything. Some things become routine, others go unnoticed, and a few small irritations can snowball into unnecessary tension. This is where the 95/5 Technique can help refocus your relationship on what truly matters.

What is the 95/5 Technique?

It's very simple:
- 95% of the Problem – The surface-level frustration (who forgot to take out the trash, the way they never close the cupboard doors, the sudden snoring that wasn't there 20 years ago).

- 5% of the Problem – The real issue underneath (feeling unappreciated, missing deeper connection, wondering if you're still growing together).

Autumn is the perfect time to slow down, shake off distractions, and focus on strengthening your relationship.

How to Apply 95/5

1. *Find the Root Issue*
   If you're suddenly annoyed at how your spouse chews their food (when it never bothered you before), it might not actually be about the chewing. Maybe it's the quiet house now that the kids are gone. Maybe you're realizing you've been focusing so much on family and work that you haven't checked in with each other in a while. Autumn invites reflection—use it to understand what's really going on.

2. *Say What You Mean*

You've been married long enough to know that "I'm fine" actually means "I am definitely not fine." Speak plainly. If something is weighing on you, say it—before it turns into a weeklong standoff about where to keep the ketchup.

3. *Listen Like You're Still Dating*

Remember how closely you used to listen to each other when you were first together? Bring that back. No multitasking, no "uh-huhs" while scrolling your phone—just genuine, undivided attention. Autumn is about appreciating what's already there; don't let familiarity turn into complacency.

4. *Make Small Adjustments, Not Big Dramas*

Fixing the real issue doesn't require a grand gesture. It's about small things—setting time aside to check in, finding a new shared interest, making space for meaningful conversation.

Real-Life Example:
The Case of the Mysterious Remote Wars

You find yourselves bickering about the TV—who holds the remote, who picks the show, and why they always fall asleep before the ending of a movie they picked. This isn't really about the remote. It's about connection.

Maybe watching TV was once a way to unwind together, but now it feels like just another habit. The solution? Turn the TV off sometimes. Go for a walk. Try something new together. Make space for fresh conversations.

Interactive Activity: The 5% Deep Dive

- *Step 1*: Each of you write down 3 things that have been annoying you lately.

- *Step 2*: Swap lists, but instead of reacting, take a moment to ask, "What's really behind this?"

- *Step 3*: Talk about how you can adjust—not just to fix the minor issue but to strengthen your connection.

Embracing Autumn with Fresh Eyes

Autumn in marriage isn't about reinventing your relationship; it's about seeing what has been there all along, with a little more clarity. By using the 95/5 Technique, you can shift your focus from what's wrong to what's meaningful, ensuring that this season brings warmth, connection, and maybe even a little laughter when you realize just how much you still have to learn about each other.

Cultivating Your Autumn Garden: Tending to the Relationship You've Grown

While summer was about growing and thriving, autumn is about tending, harvesting, and maybe even doing a little pruning.

By now, your relationship has deep roots, and you've weathered plenty of seasons together. So, let's step back and take a look at how your marriage garden is doing. Are you basking in the rewards of years of tending to each other, or do you see a few weeds creeping in that need attention?

1. What's Thriving?
(Harvesting the Fruits of Your Labor)
Take a moment to reflect—what are the strongest parts of your relationship right now?

Think of the early seeds you planted: shared values, commitments, the promises whispered in the dark. Which of those have flourished into deep trust, laughter, and a partnership that still works—even when one of you leaves the cabinet doors open every time?

- Maybe you once dreamed of traveling together, and now you find joy in spontaneous weekend road trips.
- Maybe you hoped for a strong family bond, and now you see it in the way your kids call for advice (even if they don't always listen to it).
- Maybe you just wanted a love that lasted—and here you are, still choosing each other every day.

The work you've put in has paid off—
take a moment to appreciate it.

2. Where's the Overgrowth?
(Clearing Out the Weeds)

Every garden gets a few weeds. In marriage, those weeds show up as habits we never quite fix, conversations we avoid, or routines that make us feel more like roommates than partners.

Ask yourself:
- Are we keeping our connection fresh, or are we stuck in routines that don't serve us anymore?
- Is there something we've been brushing under the rug that needs addressing?
- Do we still make time to laugh together, or has life become a long to-do list?

Pruning doesn't have to be dramatic—sometimes, a small shift in attention makes all the difference.

- Maybe you've drifted into parallel lives—what's one new thing you can do together this week?
- Maybe small annoyances have built up—what's one habit you can let go of to lighten the load?
- Maybe you're both running on empty—what's one way you can refill each other's emotional cup?

3. Keeping the Soil Healthy
(Nurturing What Matters Most)
A garden needs care beyond just planting and harvesting—it needs steady attention, even in the slower seasons.

Here's what keeps a relationship thriving through Autumn:

Communication – Not just about logistics, but real, honest check-ins.
Laughter – Because humor makes everything easier, especially when life gets serious.
Quality Time – Not just side-by-side, but fully present. Encouragement – A reminder that you still see each other's dreams.
Gratitude – For the big things, the little things, and the things you once took for granted.

A Simple Autumn Check-In: "How's Our Garden?"

Take five minutes with your partner this week and ask:

☑ What's one thing we're doing well right now?

☑ What's one thing we could do better?

☑ What's one small change that would make us feel more connected?

Because in marriage—just like in a garden—you don't have to overhaul everything to see new growth. Sometimes, a little extra attention, a little sunlight (or a well-placed compliment), and a little effort to pull a few weeds are all it takes to make the season richer.

And if all else fails, just make some cider, sit back, and admire the leaves together.

Journaling Through the
Autumn of Marriage

Autumn......the season of golden leaves, crisp air, and the realization that you and your spouse have very different opinions on thermostat settings. This is a time for reflection, transition, and maybe a little bit of rediscovery (like figuring out where your partner keeps hiding the good snacks).

Marriage in this season isn't about starting over; it's about fine-tuning what's already there. So, grab a warm drink, find a quiet moment, and dig into these journaling prompts to see what's been working, what needs adjusting, and what still surprises you about each other after all these years.

1. *The "We Didn't See That Coming" List*

Every couple has those moments where they thought, "We've got this figured out," only to find out—nope, not quite. Write down three things in your marriage that seemed manageable but turned out to be trickier than expected.

- What did this teach you about navigating change together?
- How did it shape your relationship for the better?

Example:
We thought that once the kids moved out, we'd finally get around to doing all the things we had put off for years. Instead, we spent the first six months asking each other what was for dinner—like two people who had never met before. *(Lesson: Shared purpose needs to be reinvented, not just assumed.)*

Example:
Downsizing sounded great—until we had to agree on which of our 27 coffee mugs to keep. *(Spoiler: We still have 25.) (Lesson: Compromise isn't about winning; it's about learning when to let go—and when to just quietly sneak things back into the cabinet.)*

2. The "Well, That Was Easier Than Expected"

For every unexpected challenge, there's a pleasant surprise. Think of three things you assumed would be tough but ended up being smoother than expected.

- What does this reveal about your growth as a couple?
- How did your partnership make these transitions easier?

Example:
We thought empty nesting would feel lonely, but we actually rediscovered why we liked each other in the first place. Who knew?

Example:
We were sure that aging would mean less romance, but without the chaos of raising kids, we actually have time for each other again.

4. Plan an Autumn-Themed "Us" Adventure

Your marriage is built on shared moments, so create some new ones. No need for grand gestures—sometimes, the best memories start with a simple idea. Pick one or two of these, or make up your own:

- Go apple picking, but make it a game—who can find the weirdest-looking apple?
- Take a scenic drive and stop at a diner neither of you have ever been to. Bonus points if it has a jukebox.
- Go to a fall festival and embrace your inner kids— get lost in a corn maze, try a caramel apple, or just people-watch.

- Have a backyard bonfire and trade funny or embarrassing stories from your younger years *(because laughing together is still the best kind of connection).*
- Pick a book to read together, then discuss it over a slow Saturday morning coffee *(or while debating whether the thermostat should be turned up just a little).*

Final Thought

Growing Together, Not Just Growing Older

Autumn in marriage is about appreciating the roots you've put down while still finding ways to grow. It's about recognizing that love doesn't stay the same—it deepens, shifts, and sometimes needs a little fresh air.

So, take time to reflect, laugh, and plan new adventures together. And if you still can't agree on the thermostat, well, that's what extra blankets are for.

Autumn Takeaways

Embracing the Autumn of Your Marriage

This season of marriage isn't about chasing the next big milestone—it's about soaking in what you've built, making small but meaningful adjustments, and appreciating the view. Here are some key takeaways for keeping your connection strong in this golden chapter:

1. Change is Inevitable—Face It Together

Just like the leaves, things are going to change—sometimes beautifully, sometimes messily (like when one of you suddenly decides to rearrange the entire house). The key? Adapt as a team. Transitions are easier when you remind each other: we're in this together.

2. Deepen Emotional Intimacy (Beyond "Did You Pay That Bill?")

With fewer distractions, now's the time to have real conversations—the kind that go beyond schedules and grocery lists. Talk about your dreams (yes, you still have them!), your thoughts on life, and even the things you've never quite said out loud.

3. Find Joy in Shared Adventures (Or at Least in Not Getting Lost Together)

Maybe you once traveled the world. Maybe your idea of adventure is now trying a new restaurant without checking Yelp first. Either way, keep doing things together. New experiences—big or small—keep your relationship fresh, fun, and full of stories to tell (or laugh about).

4. Reflect with Gratitude – Even for the Quirks

You've seen each other at your best and, let's be honest, at your absolute worst (morning breath included). Instead of nitpicking the small things, appreciate what's been built, what's been learned, and how far you've come. Gratitude is the secret ingredient that turns an ordinary day into something special.

5. Look Ahead—
Because the Best is Still to Come

This season isn't about looking back with nostalgia—it's about looking forward with intention. What do you want the next chapter to hold? Whether it's downsizing, learning something new, or just finally agreeing on how the dishwasher should be loaded, make plans together and move forward hand in hand.

By embracing these elements, you can navigate the Autumn of your marriage with grace, love, and a renewed sense of partnership. This season is not an end but a rich, golden chapter—one filled with wisdom, warmth, and the beauty of a love that has stood the test of time.

Chapter 4

-Winter-
Keeping the Fire Burning
Winter in Marriage -
The Greatest Reward

If you've made it to the Winter of Marriage, congratulations—you survived the heat of Summer, the unpredictability of Autumn, and now you're standing in a season that nobody really prepares you for.

In the early years, marriage is all about building—building a home, a family, a career, a life together. You run at full speed, juggling a million things, barely catching your breath. And then, one day, you wake up... and it's quiet.

The kids are grown. The career is winding down. The hustle? Slowing. And suddenly, you're sitting across from your spouse at the dinner table, staring at the same face you married 40+ years ago and realizing...

"Well, it's just us again."
Welcome to Winter.

What is Winter in Marriage?

Winter isn't about what's next. It's about what's here.

In **Spring**, *love is about discovery.*
In **Summer**, *love is about effort.*
In **Autumn**, *love is about change.*
But in **Winter**? *Love is presence.*

Winter is knowing someone so well that words aren't always necessary. . .

It's reaching for a hand in the middle of the night, just to be sure they're still there. . .

It's sitting in comfortable silence, watching the snowfall, realizing that silence is its own kind of love. . .

. . . Winter is not for the weak.

The Hard Truth About Winter

Nobody talks about how Winter sneaks up on you.

One day, you're arguing over who's driving the kids to soccer practice, and the next, you're watching those same kids drive off with moving trucks.

You spend decades building, fixing, planning, and juggling. And suddenly... all the noise disappears. The calendar isn't packed. The house is still.

If you're not careful, you'll look at your spouse and realize: We haven't really talked in years.

Here's the thing—Winter can be the loneliest season if you let it be.

Or... it can be the best season of all.

Why Winter is the Best Season of Marriage

Let's be honest—Winter comes with some changes:

- You don't move as fast as you used to.
- Your body makes sounds when you get up from a chair.
- If you bend down to tie your shoe, you look around to see if there's anything else you can do while you're down there.

But you know what else Winter brings? Freedom.

You've paid your dues. You've survived the chaos. And now? Now you get to enjoy each other again.

Winter isn't about what's ahead—it's about right now.

- Right now, you can have conversations that aren't interrupted by kids needing snacks.
- Right now, you can take trips just because you feel like it.
- Right now, you can slow down, breathe, and appreciate everything you built together.

The Myth of Love Fading in Winter

People think love fades in Winter. That's not true.
What fades is effort.

If you don't keep learning about each other, you'll wake up one day and feel like you're living with a polite stranger. But if you lean into this season—if you talk, laugh, reminisce, and dream new dreams together—Winter can be the most rewarding season of all.

Because love in Winter?
Is not about chasing something new.
It's about cherishing what's already here.

Reflection

As Sonja and I look back on our journey, we realize that it's the stories—the shared experiences, the triumphs, the failures, the ridiculous moments—that have shaped our love.

In the next section, we'll share a few of our own Winter stories—moments that tested us, strengthened us, and made us laugh when we had no choice but to laugh.

And then, we'll transition into The Relationship Check-In, a tool to help you and your partner navigate this season with intention, warmth, and maybe even a little fun.

So, grab a warm drink, settle in, and let's embrace the beauty of Winter together.

David & Sonja
SELLEY

65 Years of Love and Partnership
Story #1

The Health Wake-Up Call –
Facing Mortality Together

They say Winter in marriage is about reflection—but I'll tell you, nothing forces reflection quite like almost dying in the middle of a business meeting.

I was in New York for work, operating on a steady diet of coffee, alcohol, and stress. Eight cups of coffee a day, three martini lunches, late nights entertaining clients—you name it. I was burning the candle at both ends and lighting a few extra wicks just for fun.

Then, one day, I was in front of a room full of executives, about to make a big presentation, when suddenly... everything changed.

- The room started spinning.
- My vision went blurry.
- Voices faded in and out like a bad radio signal.

My boss, who had seen me down a week's worth of espresso in a single afternoon, yelled, "David! What the hell is wrong with you?"

That's when I knew—I wasn't invincible. I wasn't immune to time, to stress, or to the fact that my body was officially done with my nonsense.

The Call That Changed Everything

The moment I got home, Sonja took one look at me and knew something was wrong. She wasn't buying my usual "I'm fine" routine.

"David," she said, arms crossed, voice firm. "You're going to the doctor."
"I don't need a doctor."
"David."

And that was that. Appointment booked. Resistance was futile.

The verdict? If I didn't change my lifestyle, I'd be planning my own funeral. My doctor, who also happened to be my tennis buddy, looked me dead in the eye and said, "If you don't stop drinking, you'll either have a stroke or a heart attack. Take your pick."

That was the moment. I quit drinking—cold turkey—for 10 years. No more martinis, no more binge-working, no more pretending my body could handle what it used to.

And through it all? Sonja never judged me, never scolded me, never made me feel weak. She just stood by me, quietly and unwavering.

Lesson #1

Lesson Learned:
Winter Love Is About Presence

In the early years, love is **passion and excitement**. In Winter, love is **presence**—being there when the stakes are real, when life gets serious, when the years start catching up with you.

Sonja didn't try to **change me**—but she stood by me while **I changed for us.**

Story 2
The House with Memories – Letting Go of the Past
Returning to an Old Home
& Seeing Life in Reverse

There comes a time in every marriage when you stop thinking about where you're going and start reflecting on where you've been. That's Winter. It's the season when you realize that some of the best moments of your life have already happened—quietly, in the background, while you were busy living them.

For me, that realization hit hard one fall afternoon, when I found myself standing in front of our old house.

It wasn't just any house. It was the home where Sonja and I raised our kids, where we spent countless nights planning for the future, and where we learned how to build a life together. It had been decades since we'd lived there, but that house had been the backdrop of so many of our biggest memories.

The new owner—who had been living there for nearly 40 years—stepped outside and, to my surprise, said, "Would you like to come in?"

Walking Through Time

The moment I stepped inside, it was like walking through a time capsule.

- The linoleum kitchen floor still had the indentations from our old portable dishwasher.
- The bar Sonja's father built was still there, along with those naugahyde stools we thought were so classy back in the day.
- And then, I looked up...

The floral wallpaper Sonja and I had put on the ceiling—after drinking an entire bottle of wine—was still there. I had to laugh. Some of our greatest memories were hidden in the smallest details.

I ran my hand along the stair railing, remembering the nights I had carried our kids up to bed after they fell asleep watching TV. I stood in the living room, where Sonja and I once slow danced to a record player after the kids were asleep. And I smiled when I saw the backyard, the place where we had spent so many Sunday afternoons grilling, talking, and dreaming about the future.

But here's the thing about the Winter of marriage—the future you once dreamed of? You're living in it now. And nothing makes you realize that more than standing in the past.

Lesson #2

Lesson Learned:
Winter Love Is About Legacy

Love in Winter isn't about what you build—it's about what lasts.

You realize that the best parts of life aren't just in the big milestones, but in the details you leave behind.

That old house wasn't just a building. It was the story of our life—etched into the walls, buried in the floorboards, and lingering in the air. And for the first time, I realized...
We had lived a good life. And that's what mattered most.

Winter in marriage is such a powerful season, not just nostalgia, but the deep love and meaning that comes with looking back.

WINTER

The Season of Legacy
and Lasting Love

As we enter the Winter of marriage, we find ourselves in a season marked by the quiet beauty of a love that has stood the test of time. The world slows down, and so do we—less rushing, more reminiscing, and a deep appreciation for the journey we've traveled together.

Winter is not about chasing what's next; it's about cherishing what is. It's about the quiet comfort of knowing someone so well that words aren't always necessary, the laughter that still bubbles up from decades of shared jokes, and the warmth of a love that has only grown stronger with time.

This season isn't about endurance — it's about celebrating the masterpiece you've created together, embracing the joy of your shared history, and ensuring that the legacy of your love continues to shine.

With that in mind, let's pause and reflect on where we are, what truly matters, and how we can make this season the most meaningful yet.

Relationship Reflection Instructions:

• Answer each question honestly, rating from 1 (low) to 10 (high).

• Both partners should complete the assessment separately, then come together (perhaps over a cozy blanket and a favorite old song) to discuss your responses.

• There are no wrong answers—only opportunities to deepen your connection and appreciation for each other.

Let's Begin:

1. How well do we embrace the simplicity and beauty of this stage of life together? (Are we content in our winter wonderland, or still trying to run marathons in the snow?) 1/2/3/4/5/6/7/8/9/10   [   ]

2. How well do we share and relive our best memories together? (Do we cherish our history, or does one of us need a refresher on the greatest hits?) 1/2/3/4/5/6/7/8/9/10   [   ]

3. How deeply do we express appreciation for the years we've had together? (Are we wrapping each other in gratitude like a warm scarf, or taking our history for granted?)   1/2/3/4/5/6/7/8/9/10   [   ]

4. How well do we continue to adapt to the changes this stage of life brings? (Are we gracefully adjusting, or still shaking our fists at technology and doctor's appointments?) 1/2/3/4/5/6/7/8/9/10   [   ]

5. How well do we support each other's needs, both physically and emotionally? (Are we each other's greatest caregivers and cheerleaders, or do we forget whose turn it is to make tea?)
1/2/3/4/5/6/7/8/9/10   [   ]

6. How often do we laugh together and find joy in the little things? (Do we still chuckle at inside jokes, or has life gotten too serious for giggles?)
1/2/3/4/5/6/7/8/9/10   [   ]

7. How connected do we feel on a daily basis? (Are we still holding hands, or just passing the TV remote like a relay baton?) 1/2/3/4/5/6/7/8/9/10   [   ]

8. How well do we ensure that our love story is shared and remembered? (Are we preserving our legacy, or letting our love story gather dust like an old photo album?) 1/2/3/4/5/6/7/8/9/10   [   ]

9. How do we make each day special, even in small ways? (Are we finding ways to make ordinary days

extraordinary, or just waiting for the next big event?)
1/2/3/4/5/6/7/8/9/10   [   ]

10. How well are we preparing for the future together?
(Are we facing what's ahead with open arms, or avoiding the topic like an overstuffed attic?)
1/2/3/4/5/6/7/8/9/10   [   ]

Total Score: _____

Score Interpretation

- Below 50: Time to throw another log on the fire!
  Focus on rekindling appreciation and finding
  new ways to celebrate your love.
- 50 to 65: Your relationship is steady like a well-
  worn path—keep making time for connection
  and meaningful conversations.
- 65 to 85: A strong foundation! You've built
  something incredible, and now is the time to
  savor it fully.
- 85 to 100: A masterpiece in the making! Your love
  has not only endured but flourished—share your
  story, inspire others, and continue celebrating
  your journey.

Winter Reflection Prompts

1. What is one of our favorite memories, and how
    can we relive it in a small way?
2. How can we continue to surprise and delight
    each other, even in the simplest ways?

3. What wisdom have we gained from our marriage that we would want to pass on to younger couples?
4. How can we make the most of the time we have together now, without dwelling too much on the past or future?
5. What are we most grateful for in our relationship today?

Final Thought

Winter is a season of warmth—not from the outside, but from within. It's the time when love is less about grand gestures and more about the quiet, steadfast presence of a lifelong companion. It's about finding joy in the little moments, savoring the laughter, and holding on to the love that has carried you through every season.

If Autumn was about preparing for what's ahead, then Winter is about embracing what *is.* And in the end, what greater gift is there than knowing that through every challenge, every joy, and every passing year—you have built something enduring, something beautiful, something truly yours.

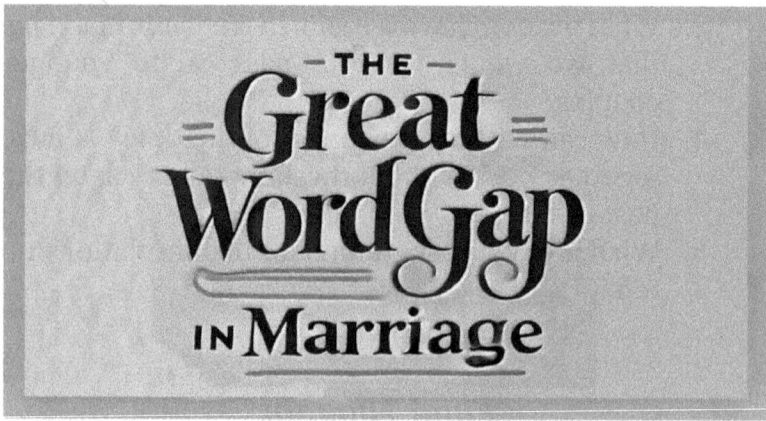

The Great Word Blizzard:

Finding Warmth in Winter Conversations

Ah, the Winter of Marriage—where the world slows, the fire crackles, and you find yourselves staring at each other across the room, wondering if you've already had every conversation possible. But let's be honest—if you've made it this far, you've certainly *said* a lot, but does that mean you've *run out* of things to say? Not a chance.

Winter isn't about running out of words; it's about making the ones you say count. It's about knowing that sometimes, a single glance speaks volumes, and other times, a well-placed "remember when..." can spark an evening of laughter. And if all else fails, there's always the weather.

Navigating the "Great Word Blizzard" of Winter

After years—decades, really—of talking about kids, careers, mortgage payments, and dinner plans, the rhythm of conversation shifts. The need for rapid-fire talks fades, and in its place, there's an eerie quiet. But don't mistake that silence for absence—it's a chance to rediscover what truly matters in your relationship.

Here's how to keep the connection alive, even when words seem to be in hibernation:

1. The Art of Saying More with Less

At this stage, you've likely mastered the art of communicating entire sentences with a single eyebrow raise. But just because you *can* doesn't mean you always *should*. Sometimes, it's worth breaking the comfortable silence to ask something unexpected:

- *"What's something you never told me about the day we met?"*
- *"If we could relive any year of our marriage, which would you pick?"*
- *"What's one thing you'd still love to do together?"*
- *"What do you think has been the best thing we ever did for our relationship?"*

Not only do these spark conversation, but they also remind you both of how far you've come—and what's still ahead.

2. The Quiet Connection: When Words Aren't Needed

By now, you know that some of the best moments don't require words at all. Whether it's sitting in comfortable silence, holding hands during a walk, or sharing a knowing look when the grandkids start acting exactly like their parents used to—you don't always need a running commentary.

But if the silence starts feeling *too* quiet, try adding a little activity to the mix:

- *A weekly "memory night" where you reminisce about past adventures.*
- *Reading the same book and discussing it over tea (or something stronger).*
- *Cooking an old favorite recipe together—bonus points if it's from a time when you both still had to read the directions.*
- *Bringing out an old photo album and seeing who can tell the best version of the same memory.*

It's not about *forcing* conversation; it's about creating space for it to happen naturally.

3. Keeping the Spark Alive (Without Setting Off the Smoke Alarm)

By now, you know love isn't just about grand gestures—it's in the little things. The morning coffee made just the way they like it. The way you instinctively reach for each other's hands. The way you still argue over the best way to load the dishwasher, even though *one of you* is clearly wrong.

To keep the spark glowing in winter:

- Surprise each other with small acts of kindness. (A handwritten note, their favorite snack, a compliment they didn't see coming.)
- Make time for just the two of you, even if it's just sitting on the couch together under a shared blanket.
- Remember that laughter is the glue of long-term love—keep finding reasons to chuckle, even if it's just at the same old jokes.

4. Looking Forward, Not Just Backward

Yes, Winter is a time of reflection, but don't park yourselves in the past. There's still more ahead!

- Plan small adventures—a weekend drive, a new restaurant, or even just a walk in a different park.
- Try something neither of you has ever done before. A class? A new game? (Just be warned— Scrabble can test a marriage.)
- Write letters to each other, reflecting on your journey together and what you still hope to experience.

Final Thought:
The Beauty of Winter Love

Winter in marriage isn't about what's lost—it's about what remains. It's about the strength of a love that has lasted through every season, every challenge, and every change. It's about the quiet certainty that, through it all, you're still here—together.

And if the conversation ever runs dry, well... there's always the weather.

WINTER

Applying the 95/5 Technique in the Winter of Marriage

Since you've made it this far together, let's be real—you already know each other's quirks by heart. The trick now is recognizing *when* to let things slide and *when* to dig a little deeper to get to the real issue. Here's how:

1. Identify the Core Issue
(Because It's Probably Not About the Thermostat)

When a disagreement pops up—say, over the *ideal* room temperature—pause for a moment. Is this really about the thermostat, or is someone feeling ignored (*or secretly plotting to move to Florida*)?

The key is to recognize what's underneath:

- Is one of you feeling like your comfort doesn't matter?
- Is this about control (because, let's face it, you've both been in charge for a long time)?
- Or is it just habit at this point to bicker about the same three degrees of warmth?

Pro tip: If the argument is older than some of your grandkids, it might be time to let it go.

2. Communicate
(Without Making It a Courtroom Debate)

At this stage, you *know* each other's go-to defenses. Instead of jumping straight into battle mode, try the direct-but-gentle approach:

- Instead of: *"You never listen to me!"*
- Try: *"When I bring something up and it gets dismissed, I feel like my thoughts don't matter."*
- Instead of: *"Why do you always leave your shoes in the walkway?"*
- Try: *"I'm worried about one of us tripping, and I'd like to avoid a hospital bill."*

It's a small shift, but it moves the conversation from blame to problem-solving (and let's be honest, that's a lot more effective).

3. Listen Like You Haven't Heard This Complaint Before (Even If You Have)

After years of marriage, it's tempting to tune out when the other person starts on a familiar rant. But *resist the urge!* Even if you *know* how the story ends, make the effort to listen anyway.

- Nodding, making eye contact, and throwing in the occasional "I see your point" can go a long way.
- And if you *really* want to impress? Respond with something unexpected—like an apology (*gasp*) or a solution.

4. Find the Humor in It (Because Let's Be Honest, It's Funny)

By now, you've got decades of inside jokes and shared absurdities. Why stop now?

Take, for example, The Case of the Wandering Eyeglasses.
Your partner has lost their glasses *again*. Instead of snapping (*because, seriously, this happens every day*), recognize the deeper truth: this isn't about the glasses— it's about change.

- Maybe they're frustrated with getting older.
- Maybe they feel self-conscious about needing more help.
- Or maybe they just like watching you crawl under the couch looking for them.

Solution? A designated glasses spot—and a good sense of humor. Instead of grumbling, turn it into a game: *First one to find the glasses gets control of the remote tonight!*

Embracing the Winter Season: Laughing Through the Layers

At the end of the day, the Winter season of marriage isn't about the little frustrations—it's about how you handle them together.

- Do you choose to laugh at the quirks instead of fighting over them?
- Do you focus on the 5% that really matters, rather than wasting energy on the 95% that doesn't?
- Do you still make each other feel important, even when life has slowed down?

Because that's what this season is really about—not just making it to the finish line, but still holding hands when you get there.

And if all else fails?
Just agree to disagree, turn on an old movie, and let the thermostat battle continue for another day.

Winter Journal: A Simple, Lighthearted Guide to Reflection in the Season of Comfort

Winter in marriage isn't about chasing big dreams or making dramatic changes—it's about enjoying what you've built, embracing what still works, and laughing at what doesn't. This season is rich with memories, inside jokes, and the simple pleasure of having someone who knows how you take your coffee (even if they sometimes still get it wrong).

Journaling together doesn't need to be an intense exercise—no essays, no overthinking. Just a chance to reminisce, reflect, and maybe even learn a thing or two about each other (yes, even after all these years).

Reflecting on Shared Experiences (Without Too Much Effort)

1. The "Oh, You Never Told Me That!" Moment
- Write down a personal story or memory you've never shared with your partner.
- Why haven't you told them before? (Be honest—did you just forget, or were you waiting for the right time?)
- Bonus points if it's something mildly scandalous from your youth.

2. Looking Back at the "Big Moments"
- Choose a major milestone in your relationship (wedding, first house, the time you tried to assemble IKEA furniture together).
- How do you feel about it now compared to when it happened?
- Would you do anything differently? (And no, "choose a different IKEA bookshelf" doesn't count.)

3. Lessons from the Tough Stuff
- Pick a challenge you've overcome together—big or small.
- How did it shape your relationship?
- What advice would you give your younger selves about getting through it? (Besides "buy the extended warranty" or "never agree to paint a room together.")

Exploring New Dimensions
(Because There's Always More to Discover)

1. The "What's Left on the Bucket List?" Chat
- Is there something you still want to do together? (And let's keep it realistic—if skydiving was ever on the list, it's okay to swap it for a scenic drive instead.)
- What's a small goal or adventure you can plan for this year?

2. Keeping the Connection Warm (Even If Your Feet Are Freezing at Night)
- What small, simple things still make you feel close?
- Are there little habits or routines you'd like to bring back? (Maybe a morning coffee ritual, holding hands more, or finally letting go of the *right way* to fold towels.)

3. Supporting Each Other's Personal Growth (Without Micromanaging)
- What's something you'd like to learn, improve, or explore in this stage of life?
- How can your partner encourage you—without signing you up for a class you never agreed to take?

Planning a Cozy Adventure (Because Fun Isn't Just for the Young Folks)

Routine is nice, but a little shake-up can make Winter feel exciting again. No, we're not talking about wild escapades (unless you want to, in which case, go for it). Think simple joys—something to look forward to, laugh about, or just enjoy together.

- Mini Getaway: A quiet weekend retreat, a day trip somewhere new, or even a staycation where you pretend you're on vacation (which mostly means ordering takeout and ignoring house chores).
- The Great Home Project (That You'll Hopefully Finish): Pick a fun little task together— reorganizing old photos, finally fixing that squeaky door, or redecorating a room. Just promise to agree on a color before going to the hardware store.
- A Culinary Experiment (or Disaster): Try cooking a new dish together—maybe even something from a place you always wanted to visit. Worst case scenario? There's always takeout.

Final Thought:
Keeping It Simple, Keeping It Fun

This season isn't about *fixing* anything. It's about enjoying what you have, appreciating the journey, and making the most of every moment—whether it's filled with conversation or just comfortable silence.

So grab a journal (or a napkin if that's closer), jot down a thought or two, and have fun with it. After all, Winter is best spent warm, together, and maybe with an extra blanket just in case.

Cultivating Your Winter Garden: Tending Love, Laughter, and the Occasional Hard Frost

The Winter of Marriage—where you've been together long enough to finish each other's sentences, predict each other's sighs, and know exactly who left the kitchen cabinet open (again). It's a season filled with deep roots, strong branches, and yes, the occasional stubborn weed. By now, you've faced life's big milestones—kids (or no kids), careers, retirement, maybe even a health hiccup or two. But let's be honest—just because you've made it this far doesn't mean it's all smooth sailing. Winter marriages come with their own set of challenges, adjustments, and unexpected plot twists.

So, how do you keep the garden thriving when the ground feels frozen, the wind kicks up a few new issues, and your knees aren't what they used to be? Let's dig in.

1. Facing New Challenges with an Old Team

Winter marriages may not have the chaos of raising kids or building careers, but don't be fooled—there's still plenty to navigate. Here are a few hurdles unique to this season:

- Health (Yours, Mine, and Ours) – Aches, pains, and surprise doctor's visits are part of the landscape now. It's no longer just "in sickness and in health," but also "who's driving to the appointment."

- The "What Did You Say?" Dilemma – Conversations are now competing with background noise, selective hearing, and an occasional battle over TV volume. Sometimes, miscommunication is less about feelings and more about needing a hearing check.

- Time Together... and *Too* Much Time Together – Retirement, slowing schedules, or changing routines can leave couples feeling closer than ever—or suddenly realizing they've run out of hobbies that don't involve each other. Finding balance is key.

- The "Who Are We Now?" Question – After decades of being a team, the roles shift. No more job titles, no more kids to raise—so who are you now, just the two of you? The good news? You get to decide.

2. Keep Planting New Seeds (Even If the Knees Aren't What They Used to Be)

A Winter Garden needs careful tending—not wild, reckless growth. The same goes for marriage. Small, steady efforts will keep things fresh.

- Try One New Thing Together – It doesn't have to be major. A new card game, a short road trip, a hobby that doesn't require too much bending down. Something fresh to talk about, even if it's just "why did we think we'd be good at this?"

- Make Plans (Even If You Have to Adjust Them) – Having something to look forward to makes all the difference. A weekend getaway, a monthly outing, or just a new tradition—because "same old, same old" isn't as fun as "something new to laugh about."

- Give Each Other a Little Space – Yes, you love each other. No, you don't need to do *everything* together. Have separate interests, even if it's just reading in different rooms and meeting up for snack breaks.

3. Navigating the Emotional Shifts

The biggest surprise about Winter marriage? The emotions don't go away just because you've been together forever.

- Facing Loss Together – Friends, family, even the

roles you once played—Winter can bring goodbyes. Leaning on each other through grief is one of the most powerful parts of this season.

- Avoiding the "Roommate Rut" – After years together, it's easy to slide into parallel living—coexisting, but not always connecting. Shake things up:

  — Surprise your spouse with their favorite treat (yes, even if it's a little salty for their blood pressure).

  — Ask new questions (or revisit old ones—"Tell me about the first time you knew we'd last").

  — Touch matters. A small hug, a warm hand on the back—it keeps the connection alive.

4. The Practical Side: Keeping the Weeds from Taking Over

Winter gardens require maintenance—so does marriage. Time to clear out the clutter, trim the unnecessary stress, and make room for what actually matters.

- Declutter More Than Just the Garage – Simplify things. Get rid of what you don't need, whether that's old grudges or that box of mystery cords.

- Talk About the "What's Next" Stuff – No one wants to talk about wills, finances, or what happens if one of you can't drive anymore. But having those conversations now gives you more peace to enjoy the years ahead.

- Celebrate What You've Built – Seriously. Take a moment to say, "Look at us. We made it this far, and we're still standing (mostly upright)."

5. Keeping the Garden Warm (And Keeping Each Other Warm, Too)

This isn't the time to stop tending to each other. A winter garden may look still, but beneath the surface, there's life—just like in marriage.

- Keep Touch Alive – It doesn't have to be dramatic. A hand squeeze, a shoulder rub, a foot tap under the dinner table. The little things still count.

- Find New Ways to Say "I Love You" – Whether it's doing the dishes before being asked, sneaking their favorite snack into the grocery cart, or just saying it out loud—don't let the words disappear.

- Laugh, Laugh, Laugh – If you're going to grow old together, you might as well be laughing the whole way.

Final Thought

This Garden is Yours—Enjoy It

Winter in marriage isn't about winding down—it's about settling in.

- The big growing seasons may be behind you, but the roots are deeper than ever.

- There's still room for new blossoms, new memories, and a whole lot of warmth.

- And best of all? You don't have to tend this garden alone.

So keep weeding out the nonsense, watering what matters, and soaking up the beauty of a love that's lasted through every season.

And if all else fails? A good blanket, a shared snack, and a little patience never hurt anyone.

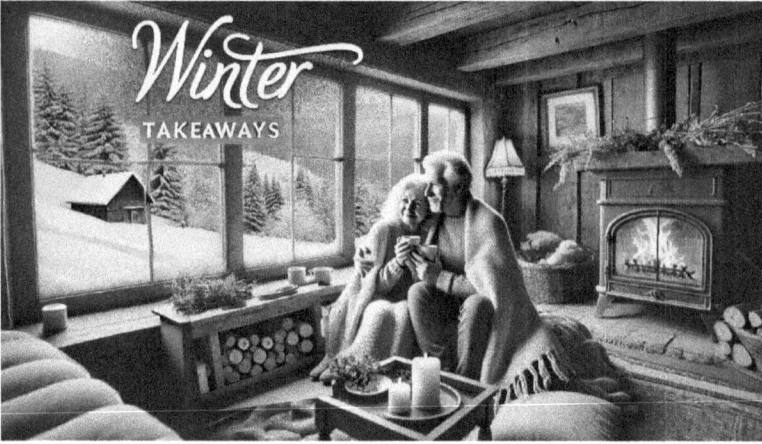

Keeping the Fire Burning ... Without Setting Off the Smoke Alarm

Winter of Marriage —where you've mastered the art of silent communication, perfected the strategic sigh, and somehow still manage to surprise each other (mostly by forgetting why you walked into the room). This stage of life isn't about fading away; it's about leaning in — into laughter, love, and the warmth of a life well-lived together.

Here are some hard-earned, practical, and slightly humorous takeaways for keeping your Winter Garden thriving.

1. Appreciate the Predictable (Because, Let's Face It, You Both Are)

By now, you know exactly what your partner is going to say before they say it—and you still listen (or pretend to).

That's love

- Find comfort in the routine, but shake it up every now and then—try a new route for your daily walk or eat dessert before dinner just to feel rebellious.
- Let the familiar be funny—if they still tell that same joke, give them a laugh. They earned it.

2. The Hearing May Go, But the Listening Matters

Selective hearing is an *underrated* survival skill in long-term marriage. But, while you may not always catch every word, make sure you catch the important ones.

- Listen like it's the first time—even if it's the tenth retelling of the same story.
- Clarify, don't assume—because "Can you hand me the remote?" and "Can you hand me a coat?" have very different consequences.

3. Keep the Laughter Alive (Even If You're the Only One Who Gets the Joke)

Laughter keeps the coldest winters warm. If you can still crack each other up, you've already won.

- Find new things to laugh about — watch a new comedy, read a funny book, or just recount the most ridiculous arguments you've ever had (*spoiler: they were all about things that didn't matter*).
- Embrace the absurdity of aging together—misplacing glasses that are on your head is a two-person sport at this stage.

5. Celebrate the Quirks (Because They're Not Changing Now Anyway)

Those little habits that used to drive you nuts? Turns out, they're the soundtrack of your love story.
- Instead of rolling your eyes, appreciate them.
- Laugh at them together—because at this point, they're probably never going away.

6. Keep the Adventures Coming (Even If They End by 8 PM)

Who says excitement ends with age? It just looks a little different now.
- Spontaneity doesn't have to mean skydiving—a random afternoon drive, a new recipe, or a completely unplanned nap still counts.
- Say yes to small surprises—try a new restaurant, explore a small town, or even just swap seats on the couch (now that's an adventure).

7. The Smallest Gestures Mean the Most

Big romantic gestures are great, but at this stage, the small things say "I love you" loudest.
- Make them their favorite tea before they even ask.
- Hold hands while watching TV.
- Leave little notes—even if they just say, "Don't forget your glasses. Again."

8. Keep Growing
(Even If It's Just Learning How to Use the TV Remote Properly)

Personal growth doesn't stop just because you've seen every possible version of each other.
- Try learning something together—even if it's just watching a documentary neither of you fully understand.
- Encourage each other's interests—even if one of you is suddenly obsessed with birdwatching and the other still doesn't see the appeal.

9. The Comfort of Silence Is a Gift
(Unless One of You Starts Snoring)

By now, you know some of the best moments don't need words.
- Enjoy the quiet companionship—no pressure to fill the air.
- Sit together, read separately, and just be.

10. Don't Get Stuck in the Past
You've built a lifetime of memories—
but don't forget to make new ones.

- Reminisce without living in "the good old days."
- Celebrate where you are now—because this is another chapter worth remembering.

11. Keep the Romance Alive
(Even If It's Less About Fireworks and More About Keeping Each Other Warm)

Romance evolves—but it doesn't disappear.
- Say "I love you" often.
- Reach for their hand, just because.
- Flirt a little — it's free, fun, and a great reminder that love is still in bloom.

Final Thought

Winter is for Enjoying, Not Just Enduring

Marriage in the Winter years isn't about fading—it's about deepening, laughing, and loving in ways that only time can teach.

So keep the fire going, tend the garden, and most importantly—enjoy every moment you have together.

And if all else fails? A good snack, a warm blanket, and a shared chuckle will get you through just about anything.

From Spring to Winter: A Marriage Well-Worn and Well-Loved. We Made It This Far – What's Next?

So, here we are. After all the seasons, all the lessons, all the self-reflection (and let's be honest, a few "discussions" about who loads the dishwasher wrong), you've made it to the end of this book. But—good news! You haven't reached the end of your marriage. Not even close.

If anything, this is just the beginning of something even better.

Because after working on yourselves, your connection, your patience (and maybe even your ability to bite your tongue when your spouse says something utterly ridiculous), life together isn't winding down—it's just getting started.

The Best Love Stories Keep Evolving

Here's something no one tells you on your wedding day: Marriage isn't a single story. It's a collection of stories—some funny, some frustrating, and some so beautiful they make the tough days worth it.

Like that time I tried to surprise Sonja with breakfast in bed and nearly burned the kitchen down. Or the time we spent a whole afternoon arguing over whether or not we *had* a favorite restaurant (we did, but apparently only one of us knew it). Or the day I walked into our old house, touched the stair railing, and was hit with a tidal wave of memories—carrying sleepy kids to bed, slow dancing in the living room, dreaming about a future that, in that moment, had already arrived.

That's the thing about marriage: Every season is filled with moments you don't realize are precious until you look back and see them for what they really were—the glue that held your love together.

And now? Now you get to take everything you've learned and step into the future, side by side, with a whole new appreciation for the journey ahead.

The Secret to "Happily Ever After"? Keep Moving Forward

........there is no finish line in marriage. No moment where you look at each other and say, "Well, we did it. Guess we can just coast from here." *Nope. Not a chance.*

Because love isn't about reaching a destination. It's about waking up every morning and choosing each other all over again. It's about:

- **Romance that still surprises you.** Yes, even after 65 years, a well-timed compliment, a lingering touch, or a love note in the middle of a chaotic day can still make your heart skip a beat.

- **Laughter that keeps you young.** Because at the end of the day, if you can't crack up at the absurdity of life together, what's the point?

- **Dreams that are still unfolding.** Who says you've done it all? There are still places to explore, projects to start, ridiculous ideas to entertain, and new ways to fall for each other.

A Marriage Well-Worn and Well-Loved

Let's be honest—your love has been through it all. The excitement of Spring, the hustle of Summer, the adjustments of Autumn, and the deep companionship of Winter. And yet, through every twist and turn, you've built something incredible:

A partnership that's stood the test of time.
A love story still being written.
A future still waiting to be lived.
So, what's next?
That's up to you.

But if I were you, I'd keep holding hands. Keep making each other laugh. Keep dreaming, keep adventuring, and for the love of all things holy, keep flirting—even if it's just a playful wink across the room.

Because when you've come this far together, the best is always still ahead.

Now go pour a drink, cuddle up, and toast to all the love yet to come. You've earned it.

Before You Say "I Do"

What Makes a Wedding Meaningful (Beyond the Event Itself)

A wedding is just one day. A marriage is every day after.

It's easy to get caught up in the excitement of the perfect ceremony, the flawless dress, the Pinterest-worthy details. But when you strip it all down, what really matters?

The commitment

Not the flowers. Not the cake. Not the seating arrangement that will probably upset someone no matter how carefully you planned it.

When I think back to our wedding day, I don't remember the little details. I remember the feeling of watching Sonja walk down the aisle, her presence so radiant that for a moment, time seemed to stop. I remember knowing—deep in my soul—that this was the person I wanted beside me for the rest of my life.

If I could give one piece of advice to engaged couples, it would be this: Plan for your marriage more than your wedding.

✓ Have the deep conversations.

✓ Talk about how you handle money, stress, conflict, and expectations.

✓ Think about how you'll support each other through seasons of growth and change.

✓ Understand that love is not just a feeling—it's a decision you make, every single day.

Because when the last guest leaves and the honeymoon glow fades, what's left is the life you're building together.

Are You Choosing the Right Person? A Pre-Marriage Readiness Check

Before you say "I do," take a moment to ask yourself:

✓ Do I like who I am when I'm with this person?

✓ Do we share the same core values and vision for life?

✓ Do we handle conflict with respect, or do small disagreements turn into battlefields?

✓ Do we laugh together? (Trust me, humor will save you more than once.)

✓ Would I still choose them if life got hard — really hard?

It's easy to be in love when everything is going well. But true partnership is built on how you handle life's curveballs together—illness, financial setbacks, losses, the unexpected realities of simply being human.

Red flags don't disappear after marriage. If something doesn't feel right now, don't ignore it, hoping it will change later.

At the same time, there's no such thing as a perfect partner. The real question isn't *"Are they flawless?"* It's *"Are we willing to grow together?"*

Choosing the right person isn't about finding someone who completes you. It's about finding someone who will walk beside you, challenge you, and bring out the best in you—through every season.

Advice for Newlyweds:
What I Wish I Had Known

I don't want to end this book until I have my final input.... even if I've repeated myself many times . . that Marriage is a beautiful, most meaningful, wild, wonderful, sometimes frustrating, and deeply fulfilling adventure. If

I could go back and give my newlywed self a few pieces of advice, here's what I'd say:

1. **You won't always feel in love**—but love isn't a feeling, it's a choice. The butterflies fade, but the commitment grows stronger when you nurture it.

2. **Your spouse isn't a mind reader.** If you need something, say it. Hinting and hoping doesn't work. Communicate clearly and with kindness.

3. **The small moments matter more than the big gestures.** The way you greet each other at the end of the day. The small "thank yous." The simple touch on the back as you walk by. These are the threads that weave a lasting love story.

4. **Laughter is your best tool for survival.** Find reasons to laugh together—even in the hard moments.

5. **Keep dating each other.** Don't let life get too busy for connection. Even if it's just a quiet walk, a slow dance in the kitchen, or a handwritten note—keep pursuing each other.

6. **Don't keep score.** Marriage isn't 50/50. Some days, one of you will carry more. Other days, the roles will switch. Give generously, without tallying points.

7. **Choose grace over perfection.** You'll both mess up. Learn how to say, *"I'm sorry,"* and mean it. Learn how to forgive, even when it's hard.

More Final Thoughts

Some Secrets to "Happily Ever After"

There is no finish line in marriage. No moment where you've "arrived."

Instead, marriage is about choosing to grow together every single day.

It's about:

✓ Learning new things about each other, even decades later.

✓ Supporting each other's dreams, no matter how small.

✓ Holding hands, even when your bodies are a little slower than they used to be.

✓ Creating a lifetime of shared memories, inside jokes, and stories worth telling.

If I've learned anything after 65+ years of marriage.....

- Love that lasts isn't about never facing challenges. It's about never giving up on each other, even when those challenges come.

- So whether you're just starting out in the Spring of marriage or reflecting in the Winter, remember:

The best love stories aren't perfect—they're simply built, day by day, with patience, laughter, and a whole lot of heart.

The end is only the beginning

The Businessman and Entrepreneur in the USA

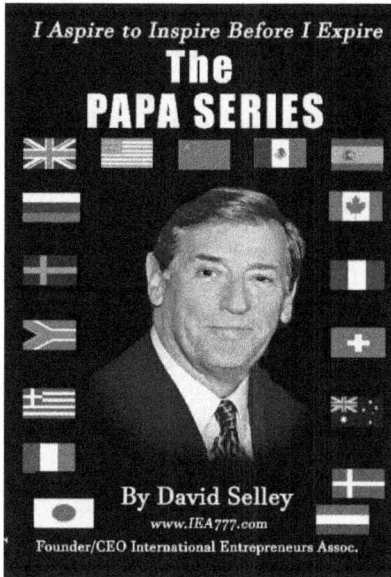

I Aspire to Inspire Before I Expire

The PAPA SERIES

By David Selley
www.IEA777.com
Founder/CEO International Entrepreneurs Assoc.

David Selley's PAPA Book Series:
A Guinness World Record Journey

David Selley's **PAPA Book Series** is more than a collection of stories—it's a testament to a life well-lived, spanning three continents and over eight decades of experiences in family, business, and personal growth. As part of his **Guinness World Record attempt to become the oldest author to publish the most books in one year**, this series captures the wisdom, resilience, and entrepreneurial spirit that have defined his journey.

From his tough childhood in England to his transformative years in Canada, and his entrepreneurial success in the USA, David's books weave together memoir, business insights, and life lessons. At the heart of the series is his 65-year marriage, a remarkable testament to love, perseverance, and partnership.

Beyond personal storytelling, David's latest entrepreneurial venture, the International Entrepreneur Association (IEA), introduces readers to a new vision for global business networking. By connecting importers and exporters in a streamlined system, David aims to create new opportunities for businesses worldwide.

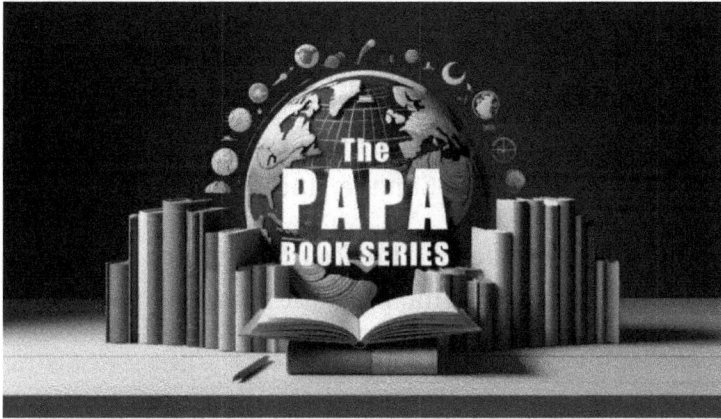

SERIES TITLES AVAILABLE NOW:

(Includes books newly released or publishing soon)

PAPA #1: **The Boy in England and Growing Up Tough** is a tale of resilience and survival from David's early days in England.

PAPA #2: The Young Man in Canada provides a look at his transformative years in Canada, filled with personal and professional growth.

PAPA #3: The Businessman and Entrepreneur in the USA chronicles David's entry into the business world and his entrepreneurial adventures in the United States.

PAPA #4: The Entrepreneur: PAPAS Secret #4 takes a deep dive into his entrepreneurial mindset and the lessons learned from building businesses.

SERIES TITLES *(continued}*

PAPA #5: Three Lives, Three Lands
A condensed journey through David Selley's life in England, Canada, and the USA

PAPA #6: Married – The Four Seasons of Marriage
reflects on the evolving phases of marriage over 65+ years, from spring to winter.

PAPA #7: How Is Your Relationship? (How to Stay Married 65+ Years)

PAPA #8: The Father explores David's journey as a
father, filled with challenges, love, and important lessons.

PAPA #9: The Grandfather – Leaving a Legacy is a
heartwarming tribute to family and the importance of passing down wisdom and values.

PAPA #10: Health, Wealth & Happiness (You Can Have All Three)
is a guide to achieving balance and abundance in life.

PAPA #11: The Investor – Nothing Down Real
Estate... Yes! It Works presents proven strategies for real estate investing without upfront costs.

SERIES TITLES *(continued)*

PAPA #12: The Famous 50 Book Series is an exciting global vanity publishing project, connecting famous people across industries at *www.famous50.com*.

PAPA #13: GenMar – The Generational Marketing Advantage reveals how understanding generational values can transform marketing and deepen customer connection.

David's Favorite Quotes

Mindset
"You can IF you think you can." – Zig Ziglar

Leadership
"Ask not what your country can do for you...
but what you can do for your country." – John F. Kennedy

Personal Development
"Change your thoughts and you change your world."
– Norman Vincent Peale

Integrity
"Try not to become a man of success.
Rather become a man of value." – Albert Einstein

Self-Belief
"Whatever the mind can conceive and believe,
it can achieve." – Napoleon Hill

Innovation
"The best way to predict the future
is to create it." – Peter F. Drucker

Critical Thinking
"People with polarized opinions will only educate
themselves to their level of ignorance." – David Selley

Practical Wisdom
"Never take advice from someone who has not
done what they are talking about." -- David Selley

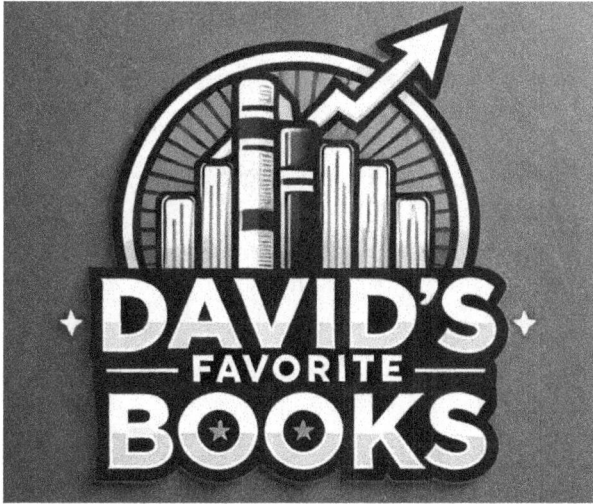

"How to Win Friends and Influence People"
by Dale Carnegie

"The Magic of Thinking Big"
by David J. Schwartz

"Think and Grow Rich"
by Napoleon Hill

"The Power of Positive Thinking"
by Norman Vincent Peale

"The Power of Focus"
by Jack Canfield, Mark Victor Hansen, and Les Hewitt

David's Favorite Books - *Continued*

"The Aladdin Factor"
by Jack Canfield and Mark Victor Hansen

"Innovation and Entrepreneurship"
by Peter F. Drucker

"Secrets of Power Negotiating"
by Roger Dawson

"See You at the Top"
by Zig Ziglar

"Live Your Dreams"
by Les Brown

The Art of Exceptional Living"
by Jim Rohn

**"Maximum Achievement:
Strategies and Skills That Will Unlock
Your Hidden Powers"**
by Brian Tracy

"The 21 Irrefutable Laws of Leadership"
by John C. Maxwell

My Creed

By Dean Alfange

*A powerful declaration of
self-reliance, entrepreneurship and personal freedom.*

I do not choose to be a common man,
It is my right to be uncommon ... if I can,
I seek opportunity ... not security.
I do not wish to be a kept citizen.
Humbled and dulled by having the
State look after me.
I want to take the calculated risk;
To dream and to build.
To fail and to succeed.
I refuse to barter incentive for a dole;
I prefer the challenges of life
To the guaranteed existence;
The thrill of fulfillment
To the stale calm of Utopia.
I will not trade freedom for beneficence
Nor my dignity for a handout
I will never cower before any master
Nor bend to any threat.
It is my heritage to stand erect.
Proud and unafraid;
To think and act for myself,
To enjoy the benefit of my creations
And to face the world boldly and say:
This, with God's help, I have done.

*All this is what it means to be an
"Entrepreneur."*

"We need someone with vision, creativity, and great marketing instincts... someone like David Selley."

-Acknowledgements-

Gratitude
FOR YOUR INFLUENCE

To the individuals listed below who I have been privileged to meet personally, I would like to publicly say "thank you" for the inspiration I received from meeting you. That inspiration has deeply impacted my life and success.
With appreciation -- David Selley

Robert Allen
Nothing Down Real Estate and Author
I bought his "nothing down" book and just did it. Later on I was grateful to be on his national infomercials and featured in his 2nd Chancers book.
www.robertallen.com

Foster Brooks
I had the pleasure of sharing 3-4 first-class flights with the comic Foster from JFK to LAX. He was genuinely funny and sincere, effortlessly entertaining the first-class cabin with his quick wit. On one occasion, I even picked up his luggage. Great memories!

Acknowledgements – *continued*

Les Brown
Famous Motivational Speaker
We met at a function in Atlanta, and I have been
inspired by his words ever since.
www.lesbrown.com

George Carlin
A close neighbor on the island in Westlake Village, CA.
George had a challenging intellect and a brilliant mind.

William (Bill) Chaplin
is a beautiful example of a "true" entrepreneur.
At the age of 18 he defied traditional customs
and pursued his dream. He now builds high
performance racing cars experiencing a multitude
of class wins and national championship honours.
If you need a custom car, contact Bill.
www.empireracingcars.com

Prince Charles, Now King of England
Then Prince Charles was the patron of the Royal Bath &
West Show in Somerset England. We met at the VIP tent
when celebrating Queen Elizabeth's Silver Jubilee. A
treasured and inspirational memory.

Rich DeVos, Founder Amway Corporation
Rich offered to help my family during a critical medical
emergency. As profit sharing Direct Distributors, I will
never forget his kindness. A truly remarkable man who
created opportunity for millions and a great company.
www.amway.com

Acknowledgements– *continued*

Elton Gallegly
Thirteen Term California Congressman
Elton was directly responsible for arranging an emergency medical evacuation for our Veteran son from Germany to Texas. I will be eternally grateful for that!

Deborah Gardner
Mrs. Arizona in 2020 and Mrs. America in 2022
is a renowned entrepreneur, author, professional aquatic swimmer, and keynote motivational speaker. She delivers powerful messages globally.
www.iamdeborahg.com

Steve Harrison
Internationally Acclaimed Media and Personal Development Expert
Steve's powerful guidance and vast media background are guiding me through the launch of my book series. I am grateful for his wisdom and knowledge.
www.steveharrison.com

Mark Victor Hansen
Co-author - The Chicken Soup Book Series (500 million copies sold!)
A powerful thought leader and transformational thinker, you have taught me how to focus on meaningful story telling. Plus, I loved being part of your exciting Enlightened Millionaire program.
www.markvictorhansen.com

Acknowledgements – *continued*

Robert Kiyosaki
Your financial wisdom, particularly in
Rich Dad Poor Dad, has shaped my financial strategies.
Thank you for that!   - *www.richdad.com*

Carol Lawrence
At 92, this famous and vibrant Broadway star, best
known for her iconic role as Maria in *West Side Story*
and numerous appearances, including seven at the
White House, continues to inspire me. She remains
sharp and down-to-earth despite her polished career.
It has been my pleasure to assist her in many ways and
she continues to inspire me with her wit, charm,
energy and positive attitude.

Ron LeGrand
Real Estate Guru
On a fishing trip to Alaska Ron gave me some great
advice "scratch the barnacles' off your brain and
release yourself to YOUR future. That was a very
powerful message from a guy who knows a lot about
real estate.   I appreciate his valuable mentorship!
www.ronlegrand.com

Bob Proctor
Great Thought Leader and
Personal Development Expert
I met Bob at an NSA event in Phoenix. He gave me
one piece of great advice that I will never forget.
"Don't let negativity into your life"
That is wonderful advice for everyone!
www.proctorgallagherinstitute.com

Acknowledgements– *continued*

Jim Rohn
Internationally acclaimed Business and Personal Development Speaker

I was on Jim's last call the day before he died from pulmonary respiratory failure. A remarkable man who has helped millions. – *www.jimrohn.com*

Mickey Rooney

Mickey lived a few doors away from us on the island in West Lake Village, California. We often exchanged pleasantries and frequent visits to the pizza parlor.

Donald Trump
President of the United States

I met Donald at a Jeff Kaller event in Orlando. He said one thing to me that has changed my life. "When you come up with an idea, pull the trigger immediately". That is what I do now! He sent my wife and I a beautiful card for our 60th wedding anniversary. A true entrepreneur and patriot!

Bud Westmore

Bud was one of the famous Westmore brothers from Universal Studios, also a devoted Anglophile. His Encino home reflected British charm, complete with a knight in armor. During lunch at his studio, he showed me the Mermaid and Psycho props. His love for England was clear in our long conversations.

Acknowledgements– *continued*

Christian Yelich
Our grandkids and Christian played together at
family parties when we lived in Westlake Village, CA.
Now, a famous MVP and Allstar baseball player.
A true inspiration for me and millions of kids.

Thank you for sharing your knowledge

*"Though we have not met personally, I want to express
my gratitude to the following individuals for their
insights and wisdom, which have been invaluable to me
in accomplishing this book series. Thank you for sharing
your knowledge with the world."*

Dale Carnegie	John Maxwell
Jack Canfield	Norman Vincent Peale
Peter Drucker	Julia Roberts
Roger Dawson	Tony Robbins
Napoleon Hill	Zig Ziglar

Contact David Selley
through www.*DavidSelley.net*
to obtain information about volume
discounts, The Step-by-Step Coaching
Programs, licensing partnership
opportunities, speaker availability.

Three lives - three countries

Regional - National – International

©2016

International Entrepreneurs Association

We provide global product distribution and entrepreneurial training through our network of Executive Directors worldwide. Though our business model is new, it is rich in experience, offering a fresh, innovative approach to global business. Our world-class team is driven by need, not greed, with a mission to help marginalized entrepreneurs reach their fullest potential. We aim to serve humanity, leaving a legacy of progress, personal growth, and upholding the highest standards of integrity and core values.

www.IEA777.com

Join Today
International Entrepreneurs Association (IEA) and Get Started for Free

As a member of the IEA, you'll gain access to a community of like-minded entrepreneurs, exclusive webinars, and my personal video series sharing the secrets to building a successful business.
Plus, as a special bonus, you'll receive
Foundations of Entrepreneurship **(a $97 value)**
absolutely free to kickstart your journey.

Go to **www.IEA777.com**
And sign up while everything is fresh in your mind.

I've walked the path you are about to take—through failure, success, and everything in between. Whether you are just starting, growing your business, or dreaming of global impact, I've created programs to meet you where you are.

Senior Parks Project

The U.S. faces a critical shortage of affordable senior housing, and Senior Parks USA aims to address this with a national chain of 100-acre parks featuring small, ergonomically designed manufactured homes for seniors. Over the next decade, the plan is to offer dignified, affordable housing to millions of seniors.

www.seniorparksusa.com

The One Day Event for Seniors
Music, Moods & Memories

The One Day Event hosted by **Long Live Seniors** is a unique, interactive experience designed to enrich the lives of seniors by offering valuable resources, expert guidance, and opportunities to connect with others in their community. Focused on promoting health, wellness, and longevity, this event is a one-stop opportunity for seniors and their families to learn, engage, and be inspired.

Event Overview

The One Day Event offers a full day of workshops, seminars, and activities tailored to the needs and interests of seniors. The event is designed to empower seniors by giving them the tools and knowledge they need to live longer, healthier, and more fulfilling lives.

www.LongLiveSeniors.com

MARR ED

David & Sonja
SELLEY

65 Years of Love and Partnership

With over 65 years of marriage, we've discovered that love is a daily decision. Our Married Program provides proven tools to help couples navigate challenges, resolve conflicts, and strengthen their bond. Using the powerful 95-5 and 1-10 techniques, you'll learn how to solve any problem and communicate effectively. Plus, uncover the 10 simple questions that can transform your relationship and deepen your connection. Whether you're rekindling the spark or building a stronger foundation, this program offers a roadmap for lasting love and harmony. Start your journey today and create your own enduring love story.

www.happylifeexpert.com

© 2016

Famous 50 Publishing Series

The Famous 50 Publishing Series offers professionals in over 100 industries the chance to join an exclusive first edition book, featuring 50 top performers. With a 4-page spread for your bio and contact details, this vanity publication is a powerful promotional tool. Gain global exposure and prestige while showcasing your expertise alongside high achievers.

www.famous50.com

About the Author

David Selley

David Selley is an international author, entrepreneur, and storyteller whose remarkable life spans over 87 years, three countries, countless ventures, and—perhaps most impressively—over 65 years of marriage to his beloved wife, Sonja.

As the author of the *Papa Book Series*, a 12-book collection combining memoir, entrepreneurial wisdom, and family reflections, David is on a Guinness World Record journey to become the oldest author to publish the most books in one year. His work blends humor, vulnerability, and hard-earned life lessons, touching readers across generations.

In *Married: The Four Seasons of Marriage*, David shares his personal insights on love, resilience, and partnership, inviting readers to explore how marriage evolves through the spring, summer, autumn, and winter seasons of life—and how to keep love thriving through them all.

Contact David Selley

www.iea777.com

davidselley08@gmail.com

1-800-388-3102

www.ingramcontent.com/pod-product-compliance
Lightning Source LLC
Chambersburg PA
CBHW071435090426
42737CB00011B/1662